Everyone knows the grill is Dad's domain. Wielding a pair of tongs and using the element of fire, he transforms raw ingredients into sizzling, delicious dishes. In *Dad's Awesome Grilling Book*, writer, father, and prolific griller Bob Sloan encourages you to dig in. Devour a few Spicy & Messy Chicken Wings. Celebrate yourself on Father's Day with some herby, satisfying Father's Day Lamb Chops. This incredibly useful cookbook also serves up helpful tips on keeping it simple when it comes to cooking tools and expert advice on choosing between charcoal and gas. With tasty recipes, sage advice, and witty reflections, *Dad's Awesome Grilling Book* is a tribute to the glory of dads and their passion for the grill.

Dad's Awesome Grilling Book

Hot

Dad's Awesome Grilling Book

Techniques, Tips,
Stories & More Than
100 Great Recipes

by Bob Sloan

photographs by Antonis Achilleos

CHRONICLE BOOKS
SAN FRANCISCO

Library of Congress Cataloging-in-Publication
Data available.

ISBN 978-0-8118-6698-9

Manufactured in China.

Prop styling by **Sara Slavin**
Food styling by **Randy Mon**
Opener Illustrations by **Laura Bagnato**

Designed by **MacFadden & Thorpe**

10 9 8 7 6 5 4 3 2 1

Chronicle Books LLC
680 Second Street
San Francisco, California 94107

www.chroniclebooks.com

CONTENTS

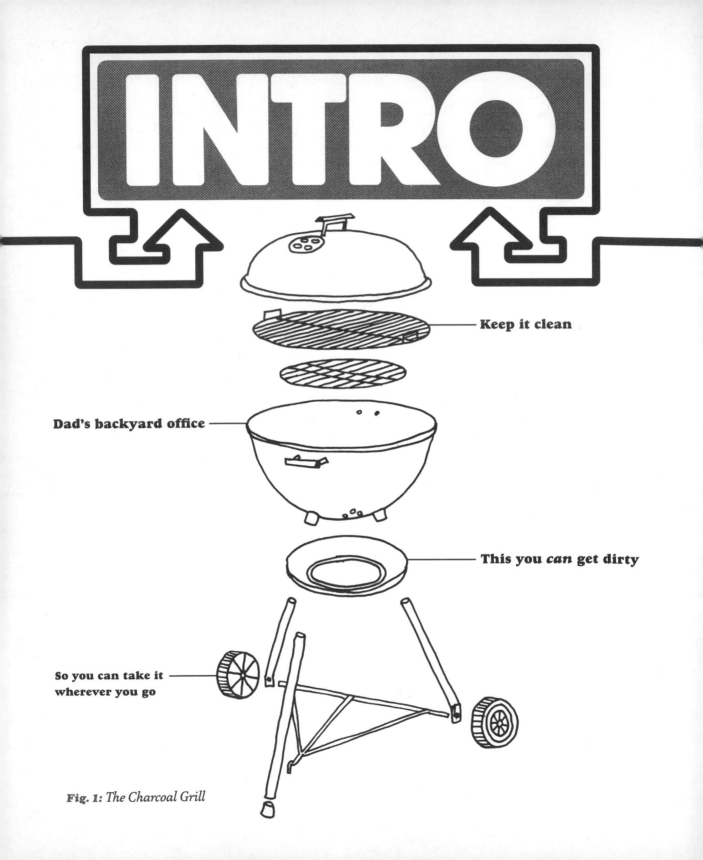

INTRO

Keep it clean

Dad's backyard office

This you *can* get dirty

So you can take it wherever you go

Fig. 1: *The Charcoal Grill*

Like so many Dads, I love to grill. Perhaps it's being so close to the fire that harkens back to an earlier, simpler time—before, say, income tax or Jerry Springer. The grill is, after all, just a man, a pair of tongs, and heat.

When the weather gets warm, when the birds start chirping and the crocus buds appear, I feel a powerful force pulling me inexorably toward the backyard. And since the hammock isn't up yet, it must be that it is pulling me to my trusty grill. For the next few months, whenever it's not raining (or at least not raining hard) I will try to cook dinner not in the kitchen, but outside on the grill. Spring means it's time for Dad to get out of the frying pan and start up the fire.

Like so many dads, I love to barbecue. When I'm standing at the grill, I'm in charge. It's my fiefdom and I'm the fief, unlike, for instance, in pretty much every other room in the house except the garage, and even there I've now been relegated to the bottom half of the shelf unit (which *I* assembled, by the way), the top being dedicated to an arsenal of paper towels, apparently, in anticipation of an oil tanker accidentally overturning on our block.

I especially enjoy having The Progeny watch me at the grill, working my magic with the charcoal. They've seen their Dad cooking plenty of times, but in the kitchen, it always feels as though something could go wrong. Cooking at the stove, I'm a bit frenetic, as if I'm always playing catch-up. At the grill, however, I'm at ease. I've got game. I'm smooth, I'm casual—as dexterous with the tongs as Chris Paul is with a basketball. I've got a good handle.

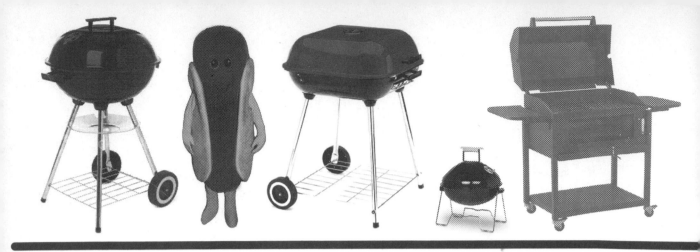

And I take everything in stride, the way a dad is supposed to. If some fat from the Chicken Thighs Cubano (page 93) hits the coals and produces a momentary burst of flame, do I flinch? Do I startle back like a rookie facing his first big league curveball? No sir. I'm calm. Relaxed. Nonplussed (or plussed—I never remember which one means dealing with adversity with casual, Dirty Harry–like disdain). Because the grill is Dad's domain, whence he fills platters with perfectly cooked burgers and ears of corn that sport their grill marks as proudly as Tom Brady does the black paint under his eyes.

And though I mean this in the nicest way, it must be said that the grill is also an oasis from Mom. Anything I cook in the kitchen is naturally compared with Mom's version. No matter how hard I try, whatever I make is either "not as good as Mom's" or "just as good as Mom's."

Either way, I'm deep in her gastronomic shadow. But the grill is Mom-proof. My efforts are compared only to the last time I barbecued, which, I have to admit, was pretty darn good.

And sometimes The Progeny even venture out and share the grill with me. There have even been afternoons when we have segued directly from the ball field to the grill, putting down our baseball mitts and donning our oven mitts as we addressed the phalanx of sizzling skirt steaks and slices of red onion for our dinner of Skirt Steak Fajitas (page 39). Or sometimes we'll stand shoulder to shoulder, mopping the Smoked Baby-Back Ribs (page 177) with their final coating of sauce or giving the Lamb and Merguez Kabobs (page 80) a final quarter-turn. If Norman Rockwell were to drive by, he would surely jam on his brakes and whip out his sketchpad.

The barbecue was made for Dad. It serves as a kind of sanctuary. Standing before the hot coals, he is insulated from spousal and parental demands that can sometimes be overwhelming. "Sorry, Honey, I can't clean up the basement now—I'm grilling!" Unlike the many vicissitudes of Fatherhood, not much can go wrong at the grill. It has few moving parts. Keep your grill grate clean and the vents open and barbecuing is simpler than checkers. Remember to fill the propane tank and you'll find there are more surprises in a game of Go Fish. The principal tool you use is a pair of tongs, which so mirrors the function of the human hand that even the most instruction-phobic dad can use them.

But most reassuring of all is how easy it is to cook on the grill. For the most part, there's step A and then there is step A again. Foolproof Burgers (page 137) require one turn after $4\frac{1}{2}$ minutes and then removal from the grill after $4\frac{1}{2}$ minutes more. Miso–Ginger Marinated Grilled Salmon (page 111) gets flipped after 5. More than culinary expertise, you need patience and decisiveness when you grill. You need resolve. It also happens to be good practice for parenting a teenager.

Equipment

Landfills across this great land are awash with sleek, colorful, leather-thonged sets of overly designed barbecue tools, none of which have a speck of grill grease on them, as they never made it out of the faux attaché case they came in. These tools may look like they've come straight from a lab at MIT, but more often than not, the spatulas are too narrow and the tongs don't grip. What's worse, they are so rigid they require the grip strength of an offensive tackle to bring them together. When it comes to grill tools, take function over form. Rest assured, even the great chefs in America grill with only a pair of aluminum tongs and the most basic of spatulas, even if they have a line of utensils with their name on them. One of the reasons dads feel at home around the grill is because of its uncomplicated efficiency. Let's keep it that way.

The Grill: Charcoal or Gas

Both charcoal and gas work great for basic grilling. If your intention is to grill a steak medium-rare with a perfectly charred out-side and a deep rosy, medium-rare center, either will work just fine. A charcoal grill is capable of producing higher heat, but you'll rarely need a fire that is quite so intense. Besides, some of the newer gas models are pumping out some serious BTUs. Most serious barbecue aficionados, however, prefer charcoal to gas. It's more intuitive. If there's a bigger pile of charcoal on one side of the grill than on the other, it's obvious which side will be hotter. But if you are the kind of person who balks at the process of lighting the coals, who will be more inclined to get out the grill if you need only turn the knob to "light," you should definitely get yourself a gas grill.

Charcoal

1. One benefit of these grills is that they impart the smoky flavor of the charcoal. This becomes even more distinct when you use real wood charcoal instead of the pressed briquettes.

2. It is much easier to add wood chips for smoking to a charcoal fire. This will allow you to further enhance the flavor when grilling over high heat or to infuse the food with the heady flavor of the wood chips by cooking slowly over indirect heat.

3. Charcoal grills allow you to cook with the top off, so you can better see the progress of the grilling.

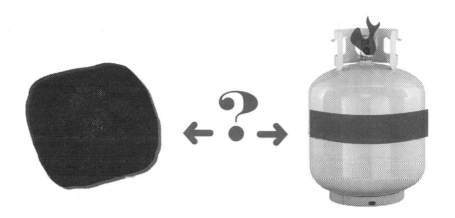

Gas

1. These grills are easier to use than charcoal ones, as there is no need to light the coals.

2. The burners may seem to be putting out even heat, but there will still be hot and cool spots on the grill. Even when new, most grill burners burn just unevenly enough to create hotter and cooler cooking zones.

3. Although with some effort you can maneuver a drip pan with soaked wood chips to sit above the burners and under the grate, smoking on a gas grill is less reliable than on a charcoal grill and is not heartily recommended. If you want to smoke foods, you're best off investing in a smoker to supplement your gas grill.

4. Most gas grills need the top to be closed in order to maintain their heat, making it somewhat harder to keep track of the progress of the grilling.

Other Equipment

Lots of serving bowls and platters
(Having a few too many will only make your grilling life easier—remember, you can't bring the cooked food into the house on the same platter you brought the raw food out on unless you take the time to clean it or it's a platter of tofu.)

Several large serving spoons

Chimney-style charcoal igniter

2 cutting boards

1 chef's knife, 1 serrated knife

1 paring knife

4 mixing bowls

Long-handled tongs

Spatula and fish spatula

2 small saucepans for reheating on the grill

Cast iron skillet for cooking on the grill

Can opener, church key, and corkscrew

Lots of paper towels

Matches or lighter fluid–filled match thing

Prep table, 3 to 4 feet long and situated by the grill

Grilling Basics

Grilling is an art. Each time you fire up the barbecue is different. You'll need to feel out the hot spots and rotate the food to and from those areas so everything will be done at the same time. Remember, the grill doesn't do the cooking. You do the cooking. The grill just gets hot.

How Hot is Hot?

If you're using a gas grill, you can simply turn the knob to the desired setting. With charcoal it's a bit trickier. The best way should be familiar from your touch football days. Simply hold your hand about 3 inches over the grilling grate and count Mississippis until the heat forces you to pull your hand away.

3 Mississippis = medium-hot fire
2 Mississippis = hot fire
1 Mississippi = *very* hot fire

For a kettle-style grill, a tightly packed single layer of coals will usually yield a medium-hot fire. Adding about a third more coals will make a hot fire.

Here are some tips to keep in mind:

1. Wait for the coals to heat up. Coals achieve optimum heat when they are completely ashed over, usually about 20 minutes after lighting. If you are grilling any appetizers, you may need to add more coals to the pile before grilling the main course.

2. For gas grills, don't forget the gas. Nothing is more humiliating than watching your flame sputter out and fail just as the steaks hit the grill. (And dads, they don't yet make a little blue pill to solve this problem.)

3. Know when to use the cover. Most cooking on a gas grill is done with the cover down. With charcoal, it depends on what you're grilling. For steaks, burgers, or any cut of meat, poultry, or fish requiring a short time over a hot fire, cook with the cover off. Anything cooked slowly off the heat will require the grill to be covered. Always position the vents on the cover over the food—this draws the heat and smoke to that side of the grill. Use the cover of your charcoal grill briefly to keep flare-ups under control—covering the grill for 10 seconds or so should put out the flames.

4. Keep your grill clean. The best way to do this is to use a wire brush right after you finish cooking. The cooking grate is hot, and the grease will come off easily. Maintaining a clean grill is not just a fussy step that you can ignore—it prevents the food from sticking to the grate.

5. Use tongs or a spatula to turn food on the grill. Never use a fork, which only serves to release the precious juices from the meat.

6. Apply sauces or marinades to meat during the last few minutes of cooking to keep from burning them.

7. The platter you use to bring the uncooked food to the grill is *not* the platter you use to bring the cooked food to the table unless you *wash it well* with hot, soapy water. It's always best to have two platters, one designated for the raw food and one designated for serving. That way, when the chicken is ready to come off the grill, you are not scrambling around for a serving platter and being tempted to say, "What the heck—I'll use the one I brought the chicken out on—just one time won't hurt anybody."

8. Always make a little more than you think you'll need. Somehow, food fresh from the grill has a way of disappearing.

Don't Start the Party Without Me

THERE WAS A PERIOD when my 10-year-old was having a very hard time falling asleep. It wasn't monsters keeping him up. It was just the opposite. He couldn't sleep because he was convinced that once he conked out, I and his mom and his older brother would break out the champagne and root beer and chocolate cake and start having a party.

"I hate being the youngest," he would say, forcing his eyes to stay open. "It's totally unfair!"

He'd managed to convince himself that ice cream sundaes of mammoth proportions were being consumed as soon as he closed his eyes. That the three of us would play cards, hold marathon Monopoly games, put on the CD of *West Side Story* and act out all the parts. All without him! We never went to bed. Our night was one long celebration. Not only that, but LeBron would just happen to stop by, along with Tintin and Snowy and Ronaldinho, the soccer star.

It didn't matter that if he snuck out of bed and surreptitiously checked on us, he found only his brother studying French, his mom doing her reading for her book group, and me in the kitchen finishing up the last of the dishes from dinner. That, too, was just another trick, as in the Sinatra movie *Robin and the Seven Hoods*, when the casino magically transforms into a library whenever the cops show up.

"You all can't wait for me to fall asleep," he would declare, "so you can start having fun!"

And all I could do was smile and say to him, "Son, I only wish it were true."

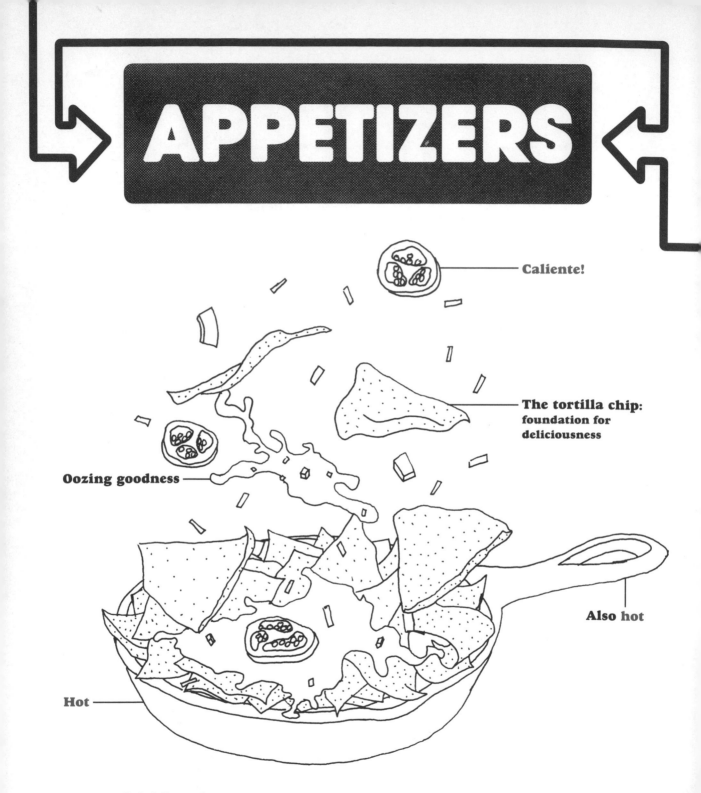

APPETIZERS

Caliente!

The tortilla chip: foundation for deliciousness

Oozing goodness

Also hot

Hot

Fig. 2: *Grilled Skillet Nachos*

02

"Isn't it enough," you say, "isn't it enough that I am working my butt off to grill a fabulous main course, and now you tell me I have to make appetizers, too?? That's outrageous."

And indeed it would be if I had not carefully selected these particular appetizers, all of which can be made ahead or require little supplemental preparation.

When you're cooking just for the family, an appetizer course definitely isn't *de rigueur* or any kind of *rigueur*, though some, like Spicy Steak Sticks (page 19), are so easy that they don't seem like much extra work. But when guests drop by, assuming that you've invited them, having an appetizer or two is an essential part of the meal plan. People have an annoying habit of arriving to a dinner party hungry. You would think they would be considerate enough to eat before they get there, but *no*. So you need something to feed them when they first arrive, to keep them mollified while you do the final prep work for the main course. People also like to nosh on something while they are drinking.

Sometimes, at our house, the appetizers can become the main course. I just double up on the Korean Short Ribs (page 24) and make that the meal. And if the kids are still hungry after that, Let Them Eat Cereal.

Scallops & Prosciutto on Rosemary Skewers

Because scallops cook so quickly, you can use rosemary sprigs as the skewers. This not only looks cool to The Progeny, but also gives the scallops an infusion of rosemary flavor while they grill. They also make a nice impression with the guests. And pruning the twiggy sprigs for their "skewers of duty" is definitely something The Progeny can be responsible for. **Serves 6 as an appetizer**

Ingredients

6 fresh rosemary sprigs, each 4 inches long

4 ounces prosciutto, sliced paper-thin

12 sea scallops, crescent-shaped membrane removed

3 tablespoons extra virgin olive oil

1 lemon, cut in half

Salt and freshly ground black pepper

→ **Strip** the leaves off the bottom 2 inches of each rosemary sprig, exposing the woody stem. Cut the prosciutto slices in half lengthwise. Wrap a piece of prosciutto around each scallop. Skewer the scallops crosswise with the rosemary sprigs, 2 scallops per sprig, making sure to skewer the prosciutto as well. Arrange the skewers on a platter. Drizzle both sides with olive oil, squeeze lemon juice over them, and season to taste with salt and pepper. Let stand while you prepare the fire.

Prepare enough coals for a hot charcoal fire, or preheat your gas grill on high for 10 minutes with the lid closed.

When the coals are ready or the gas grill is hot, grill the scallops for 3 minutes. Turn and grill for 2 to 3 minutes more, until they are just cooked through.

Serve immediately.

Spicy Steak Sticks

Barbecue sauce with a touch of heat always seems to put The Progeny in a good mood. These skewers also cook quickly enough that you won't use up all the heat of your charcoal on the appetizers. **Serves 6 as an appetizer**

Ingredients

½ **cup medium-hot barbecue sauce or Spicy Barbecue Sauce (page 21)**

¼ **cup fresh lemon juice**

2 **tablespoons vegetable oil**

¾ **pound flank steak, cut across the grain into ½-inch strips**

One **1-ounce package fajita seasoning**

12 **long bamboo skewers**

→ **In** a small bowl, stir together the barbecue sauce, lemon juice, and oil.

Place the steak strips in a large bowl and add the fajita seasoning. Toss until all the pieces are lightly coated. Add the sauce and stir to coat all the steak pieces. Let sit at room temperature for 30 minutes, or refrigerate for up to 8 hours.

One hour before grilling, soak the skewers in warm water.

Prepare enough coals for a hot charcoal fire, or preheat your gas grill on high for 10 minutes with the lid closed.

While the coals are heating up, thread 2 strips of steak onto each skewer, keeping them as stretched out as possible. When the coals are ready or the gas grill is hot, grill the steak skewers for 6 to 7 minutes, turning once, until they are just cooked through.

Serve immediately.

Spicy & Messy Chicken Wings

In the culinary world, when the words "spicy" and "messy" are used together, it can only mean something glorious. These wings are actually more messy than spicy, so you won't need the CSI unit to let you know where your kids have been after they eat them. **Serves 6 to 8 as an appetizer**

Ingredients

2 tablespoons chili powder

2 tablespoons paprika

1 tablespoon garlic powder

1 teaspoon salt

½ teaspoon cayenne pepper

½ teaspoon ground cumin

¼ teaspoon ground cloves

24 chicken wings

3 tablespoons extra virgin olive oil

Spicy Barbecue Sauce (recipe facing page)

➔ **In** a small bowl, combine the chili powder, paprika, garlic powder, salt, cayenne, cumin, and cloves and stir together. Trim off the small portion from each wing and discard. Cut the remaining wing in half at the joint. Place the wings in a large bowl, add the spice mixture, and toss to coat the wings evenly. Add the olive oil and toss again. Cover the bowl or transfer the coated wings to a resealable freezer bag and refrigerate for 1 hour or up to 4 hours.

Prepare enough coals for a medium-hot charcoal fire, or preheat your gas grill on medium-high for 10 minutes with the lid closed.

When the coals are ready or the gas grill is hot, arrange the wings on the grate in neat rows. Grill them for 8 minutes, turn, and grill for 7 to 8 minutes more, until they are just cooked through. Slather Spicy Barbecue Sauce onto the wings and turn them several times during the last few minutes of cooking so they are covered with a thick, unctuous, and delectable coating of sauce.

Transfer the wings to a platter and serve with lots of napkins.

Spicy Barbecue Sauce

A fast, all-purpose barbecue sauce that's a little on the thick side, making it perfect to get these wings good and messy, with the emphasis on *good*. **Makes 1 cup**

Ingredients

3 tablespoons tomato paste

½ cup ketchup

¼ cup fresh orange juice

2 tablespoons molasses

1 teaspoon garlic powder

1 teaspoon chili powder

½ teaspoon red pepper flakes

¼ cup brown sugar

1½ teaspoons kosher salt

½ teaspoon freshly ground black pepper

→ **In** a medium mixing bowl, stir together the tomato paste, ketchup, orange juice, molasses, garlic powder, chili powder, red pepper flakes, brown sugar, salt, and pepper until well combined. Set aside until ready to use or store, refrigerated, in a well-sealed container for up to 2 weeks.

Barbecued Wings Charlotte Style

Barbecuing is seductive. Besides the obvious lure of the food, there is the whole barbecue culture thing. The more time you spend at the grill, the more susceptible you are to being pulled into it. For instance, these wings are mopped with a classic Carolina barbecue sauce, which gets its distinctive flavor from the addition of vinegar. Soon you will be able to tell all the styles apart. After that, you'll find a way to turn the broken clothes dryer into a smoker. **Serves 6 to 8 as an appetizer**

Ingredients

24 **chicken wings**

2 **cups apple cider vinegar**

¾ **cup tomato paste**

¼ **cup ketchup**

3 **tablespoons brown sugar**

1 **tablespoon vegetable oil**

1 **tablespoon Worcestershire sauce**

1 **teaspoon red pepper flakes**

1 **teaspoon salt**

→ **Trim** off the small portion of each wing and discard. Cut the remaining wing portions in two at the joint and place in a medium pot. Add the cider vinegar, tomato paste, ketchup, brown sugar, oil, Worcestershire sauce, red pepper flakes, and salt and bring the liquid to a boil over medium-high heat. Immediately reduce the heat to medium-low and simmer the wings for 15 minutes. They should be just cooked through.

Let the wings sit in the pot while you get the grill heated up, or cover and refrigerate for up to 24 hours.

Prepare enough coals for a medium-hot charcoal fire, or preheat your gas grill on medium-high for 10 minutes with the lid closed.

When the coals are ready or the gas grill is hot, arrange the wings on the grate in neat rows and grill for 8 to 10 minutes, until they are nicely browned, turning them a few times and mopping liberally with the leftover sauce from the pot during the last few minutes.

Transfer the wings to a platter and serve with lots of napkins.

Spices? We Don't Need No Stinkin' Spices

OH YES YOU DO. Dad seasons. Get used to it. That drawer in the kitchen with all those insidious little bottles nestled cozily together, the drawer you pay about as much attention to as the one that houses vacuum cleaner bags, *that* drawer is now going to be an integral part of your world. You will know it intimately, the way you know your collection of CD's or the bent corners of your Derek Jeter rookie card.

But Dad doesn't need to know every spice. In fact, the majority of what resides in most kitchen spice drawers should be summarily discarded, like that compilation CD of '70s Glam Rock you got just for the Mott the Hoople single that wasn't nearly as good as you remembered. Allow me to help you perform some spice drawer triage.

The only green stuff you need in there are the following: bay leaves, rosemary, oregano, sage, and thyme. These are the few herbs that, when dried, can still impart some degree of flavor to the dish they are used in. Any others—mint, parsley, dried chives, basil—have little or no impact, not to mention that most people's spice jars are months, if not years, out of date. These herbs should be used fresh or not at all.

But the other jars, not the herbs but the *spices*, most of them a musky shade of rust or brown or dull green, are essential to grilling. Spices such as paprika, chili powder, cumin, and allspice are mentioned frequently in these and many other grilling recipes. Along with sugar and salt, they will be the components of your dry rubs. They will also factor into your braising liquids and your barbecue sauces. Though the best spices are the result of freshly grinding the seeds, you can get a fair approximation of those redolent flavors by buying ground spices at a reputable market and assiduously replacing them every year, whether you have used them up or not.

So now for your birthday, in addition to the dozen golf balls and the DVD of *Barbarella*, ask for some new spices. A really good chili powder. A special down-home rub mixture. And your very own set of measuring spoons, which you can use until you feel cavalier enough to just eyeball it. What more could a dad want?

Korean Short Ribs

Buy the small pieces of short rib, ones that the butcher has cut across the bone into about 1-inch sections. They cook fast and, once they make it to the platter, they're gone just as quickly. **Serves 6 to 8 as an appetizer**

Ingredients

1½ cups white wine

¾ cup soy sauce

1 bunch scallions, green parts only, finely chopped

3 tablespoons coarsely chopped fresh ginger

8 cloves garlic, coarsely chopped

6 tablespoons brown sugar

1 teaspoon Chinese five-spice powder

4 pounds beef short ribs

→ **Combine** the white wine, soy sauce, scallions (reserve ½ cup for garnish), ginger, garlic, brown sugar, and five-spice powder in a Dutch oven. Add the short ribs and bring the liquid to a simmer over medium-high heat. Immediately reduce the heat to low, cover the pot, and simmer the short ribs for 1 hour.

Using a slotted spoon, transfer the ribs to a bowl or plastic container. Skim the fat from the cooking liquid and pour the liquid back over the ribs. The ribs can be cooked to this point up to 2 days before grilling. Store them, covered, in the refrigerator and bring to room temperature before grilling.

To finish the ribs, prepare enough coals for a hot charcoal fire, or preheat your gas grill on high for 10 minutes with the lid closed.

When the coals are ready or the gas grill is hot, arrange the ribs on the grill so they aren't touching, and grill for 7 to 8 minutes, until they are slightly charred outside and heated through in the center. Turn the ribs several times, mopping each time with the leftover sauce.

Transfer the ribs to a platter and serve hot or at room temperature, garnished with the reserved chopped scallions.

Prosciutto-Wrapped Grilled Asparagus

The Progeny can definitely help prepare this simple yet elegant appetizer. Once you've grilled the asparagus, they can drape each stalk gracefully with a swath of prosciutto and then arrange them neatly on a platter. **Serves 6 as an appetizer**

Ingredients

2 pounds asparagus, medium to thick (about ½ inch in diameter; see Note)

2 tablespoons extra virgin olive oil

Salt

8 ounces prosciutto, thinly sliced

→ **Snap** off the bottom of each asparagus spear; it should obediently break off right where the woody part ends. Peel the bottom 3 inches with a vegetable peeler.

Place the asparagus in a single layer on a platter or baking sheet. Brush with olive oil and sprinkle with salt to taste.

Prepare enough coals for a hot charcoal fire, or preheat your gas grill on high for 10 minutes with the lid closed.

When the coals are ready or the gas grill is hot, lay the asparagus spears across the grate, so they won't fall into the fire, and grill until they are lightly brown all over, 4 to 5 minutes.

Transfer the asparagus to a platter and let cool to room temperature.

Cut the prosciutto slices in half lengthwise and wrap one around the center of each asparagus stalk. Arrange the wrapped asparagus on a serving platter and serve.

Note: *You can use thin or thick asparagus for this dish. Trim the thinner spears with a knife instead of snapping them. They cook very fast and should be ready after just 3 or 4 minutes.*

Grilled Apricot Salsa

This is the ideal appetizer. Set it out in a bowl and put a bag of chips next to it. Everyone knows the drill. **Makes about 1 cup**

Ingredients

4 **ripe apricots, cut in half and pits removed**

Spray cooking oil

½ **medium onion, peeled and cut widthwise into ½-inch slices**

1 **red bell pepper, stemmed, seeded, and cut into 1-inch pieces**

8 **Roma tomatoes, chopped (see Note)**

3 **scallions, green parts only, finely chopped**

¼ **cup cilantro leaves**

1 **tablespoon fresh lime juice**

2 **teaspoons chili powder**

1 **teaspoon ground cumin**

1 **teaspoon salt**

Dash Tabasco or other favorite hot sauce

Tortilla chips, for serving

→ **Prepare** enough coals for a hot charcoal fire, or preheat your gas grill on high for 10 minutes with the lid closed.

While the grill is heating up, arrange the apricot halves on a platter, cut sides up, and spray them liberally with oil.

When the coals are ready or the gas grill is hot, grill the apricots, cut sides down, for 4 to 5 minutes, until they are a deep golden brown. Spray the tops with oil and use a spatula to turn them over. Grill for 2 minutes more, then transfer to a platter and let them cool.

Place the onion, bell pepper, Roma tomatoes, scallions, cilantro, lime juice, chili powder, cumin, salt, and Tabasco into the container of a food processor, along with the cooled apricots, and pulse until finely chopped but not smooth.

Transfer to a bowl and serve with tortilla chips.

Note: *If you can't find any decent fresh tomatoes, you can substitute canned whole tomatoes.*

Queso Fundido

This Mexican cheese concoction is so intensely flavorful it'll quickly become your family's favorite fondue. And if it happens to be your *only* fondue, that's okay too. If you don't have an official fondue pot sanctioned by the A.S.P.C.F. (American Society for the Prevention of Cruelty to Fondue), you can serve the mixture in the saucepan you initially fondued it in, reheating the mixture briefly on the grill when it gets too stiff. **Serves 8 to 10 as an appetizer**

Ingredients

1 cup white wine

8 ounces mozzarella cheese, grated

8 ounces Monterey Jack cheese, grated

8 ounces soft goat cheese, crumbled

4 ounces thinly sliced capicolla or smoked ham, finely chopped

One 4-ounce can chopped green chiles

2 cloves garlic, peeled and finely chopped

Salt and freshly ground black pepper

Tortilla chips, for serving

→ **Prepare** enough coals for a two-tiered fire, hot on one side, medium on the other, or preheat your gas grill on medium-high on one side and medium on the other for 10 minutes with the lid closed.

When the coals are ready or the gas grill is hot, place a medium saucepan on the hot side of the grill, add the wine, and bring it to a simmer. Immediately transfer it to the medium side of the grill, add the mozzarella, Jack, and goat cheeses, and stir continuously until the cheese is melted. Stir in the capicolla, green chiles, garlic, and salt and pepper to taste and simmer for 2 minutes.

Transfer the mixture to a fondue pot and let it cool down a bit before serving with the tortilla chips.

Grilled Skillet Nachos

These feral nachos prepared on the grill are easier to make and, for some reason, better tasting than the tamer, domesticated version heated in the oven. You can allocate the responsibility of nacho assembly to The Progeny. Let them make an art project out of it, and then have them bring you the completed skillet for its final heating on the grill. **Serves 6 as an appetizer**

Ingredients

8 ounces tortilla chips

12 ounces Monterey Jack cheese, grated

One 12-ounce jar salsa

One 4-ounce can chopped green chiles

One 4-ounce can chopped jalapeño chiles

➜ **Prepare** enough coals for a hot charcoal fire, or preheat your gas grill on high for 10 minutes with the lid closed.

While the grill is heating up, arrange the tortilla chips in a large cast iron or other oven–safe skillet. Top the chips with the grated cheese. Spoon the salsa over the cheese, distributing it evenly. Scatter the green chiles and jalapeños over the top.

When the coals are ready or the gas grill is hot, place the skillet on the center of the grill. Cover the grill and let the nachos heat up until the cheese has melted, 4 to 6 minutes. Remove the pan from the heat and serve the nachos in the skillet, making sure you put a hot pad over the handle so no one grabs it by mistake.

Note: *If you don't have an appropriate skillet that can go on the grill, make a kind of schooner out of doubled–up aluminum foil and use that instead.*

Grilled Red Pepper Hummus Dip

It's important to teach The Progeny how to make hummus, as it will become one of their staples in college when they finally get their own place to live. If you are grilling up some peppers for another recipe, roast an extra one for this.
Makes about 1½ cups

Ingredients

1 red bell pepper

One 15-ounce can chickpeas, drained

2 tablespoons extra virgin olive oil

2 tablespoons tahini

1 tablespoon fresh lemon juice

1 clove garlic, coarsely chopped

½ teaspoon salt

¼ teaspoon cayenne pepper

4 pita breads, each cut into 8 wedges, for serving

2 carrots, peeled and cut into 4-inch spears, for serving

→ **Prepare** enough coals for a hot charcoal fire, or preheat your gas grill on high for 10 minutes with the lid closed.

When the coals are ready or the gas grill is hot, grill the red pepper for 8 to 9 minutes, turning it until it is evenly blackened all the way around.

Transfer the pepper to a medium bowl, cover with a plate or pot lid, and let it rest for 20 minutes to continue cooking.

Peel the black skin from the pepper, then slice it open and remove the stem and seeds. Cut the pepper into roughly 1-inch pieces.

Place the pepper, chickpeas, olive oil, tahini, lemon juice, garlic, salt, and cayenne in the container of a food processor or blender and pulse just until the mixture is smooth. Taste and correct the seasoning, if necessary.

Transfer to a medium bowl and serve with the pita wedges and carrots.

Spanish Potato Tortilla

This traditional Spanish dish is a prime cooking lesson for Dad, as you discover how the simplest of ingredients—potatoes, onions, and eggs—can be transformed through proper use of heat into something transcendent. If you serve this *sans* children, pop open a bottle of prosecco to go with it. **Serves 6 as an appetizer**

Ingredients

2 pounds Yukon Gold potatoes, peeled and sliced ¼ inch thick

10 large eggs

Salt and freshly ground black pepper

¼ cup extra virgin olive oil

1 large onion, halved lengthwise and thinly sliced crosswise

→ **In** a large saucepan, cover the potatoes with cold water and bring them to a boil over high heat. Reduce the heat to moderate and simmer until the potatoes are just tender, about 7 minutes.

Drain the potatoes and rinse under cold running water to stop the cooking, then let them drain again. Spread the potato slices on paper towels and pat dry.

Prepare enough coals for a two-tiered fire, hot on one side, medium on the other, or preheat your gas grill on high on one side and medium on the other for 10 minutes with the lid closed.

While the coals are heating, lightly beat the eggs in a large bowl. Stir in the potatoes and season generously with salt and pepper.

When the grill is hot, place a heavy 12-inch cast iron or other oven-safe skillet on the hot side of the grill. Add the oil. Add the onions and cook, stirring often, until golden brown, 4 to 6 minutes.

Add the egg mixture and cook, stirring gently but continuously, until the bottom third of the eggs are set, about 2 minutes.

Transfer the skillet to the medium side of the grill, cover the grill, and let the tortilla cook for about 12 minutes, or until the eggs are set and the tortilla is lightly browned. After 6 minutes, turn the skillet so the opposite side faces the high heat.

Remove the skillet from the grill and let the tortilla cool for 2 minutes.

Loosen the tortilla from the pan by running the tip of a thin spatula around the edge. Place a round platter over the pan and invert. Cut into wedges and serve.

Grilled Poblano Pepper, Cheddar Cheese & Black Bean Dip

One doesn't usually think of dads and dips in the same breath. Indeed, one of the reasons to become a dad is that you are exempt from dip preparation. If dip appears, a dad might, well, dip. If not, no great loss. But this particular dip is dad-worthy. It is stalwart. It has fortitude. And if you feel a hankering for it and don't have any immediate grilling plans, you can easily roast the pepper directly over the flame on your gas stove. **Makes about 2 cups**

Ingredients

1 good-sized poblano pepper

One 12-ounce can black beans, drained

½ cup cilantro leaves

1 teaspoon chili powder

½ teaspoon ground cumin

1 teaspoon salt

½ teaspoon cayenne pepper

4 ounces extra-sharp Cheddar cheese, grated

½ cup finely chopped scallions, green parts only, plus 2 tablespoons for garnish

Tortilla chips, for serving

→ **Prepare** enough coals for a hot charcoal fire, or preheat your gas grill on high for 10 minutes with the lid closed.

When the coals are ready or the gas grill is hot, grill the poblano pepper for 8 to 9 minutes, turning it until it is evenly blackened all the way around.

Transfer the pepper to a medium bowl, cover with a plate or pot lid, and let the pepper rest for 20 minutes to continue cooking.

Peel the black skin from the pepper, then slice it open and remove the stem and all seeds. Cut the pepper into roughly 1-inch pieces.

Place the pepper, black beans, cilantro, chili powder, cumin, salt, and cayenne in the container of a food processor and pulse just until the mixture is smooth.

Transfer the bean mixture to a medium bowl and stir in the Cheddar cheese and ½ cup scallions. Serve garnished with 2 tablespoons chopped scallions and with tortilla chips for dipping.

The Double Standard

AN UNPRECEDENTED AMOUNT of scrutiny is placed on Dad whenever he attempts to cook. We are definitely held to a different set of standards. Dads have to be eternally diligent, always maintaining a sense of culinary decorum. People may not want to hear this, but the bitter truth of the matter is, Dad will always be judged differently in the kitchen, for no other reason than the simple fact that he is a man.

Take dips, for instance. Moms across America can, with impunity, come up with bizarre and wacky dip concoctions that fill the pages of local church and community cookbooks, and they are perceived as "charming" or "down-home" recipes. Even such abstract assemblages as "Beer and Roquefort Cheese Dip" or "Pineapple-Onion Cheese Balls" are lauded as "authentic" and "genuine" regional fare. NPR would do a feature story—The Cheese Balls of Authentic County—and in sanctimonious tones interview these courageous women who are so valiantly keeping the local cheese ball tradition alive.

But if a *dad* tried to champion recipes such as these, his efforts would be labeled "ludicrous," "inedible," and "totally out of touch with the times." Far from preserving time-honored down-home traditions, he would be seen as completely out of date, making lard-laden, absurdly flavored dishes that have no place in our refined and brave new culinary world.

But we dads persevere. We suffer the doubting looks, the derisive asides whenever we bring a platter of grilled chicken wings to the potluck or a container of homemade cookies for the soccer game snack.

We know it can't last forever, that this last insidious vestige of an outmoded set of values will eventually disappear. And every dad who takes the time to prepare dinner does his bit to chip away at the glass kitchen ceiling. Some day it will be a thing of the past, like those rubber tubes that looked like cannoli and were supposed to make peeling garlic a cinch—try to find one of *those* now.

Grilled Crab Cakes with Chipotle Mayonnaise

It may not seem prudent to cook something as delicate as a crab cake on the grill, but it works. The trick is to let them sit for at least 2 hours in the fridge, which helps them maintain their integrity while they are cooking and, as usual with fish, to coat them liberally with cooking spray before grilling. The result is the perfect crab cake.

Serves 4 as an appetizer

Ingredients

1 pound lump or backfin crabmeat, drained and picked over for shells

¼ cup chopped scallions, green parts only

¼ cup breadcrumbs

1 egg, beaten

3 tablespoons mayonnaise

2 teaspoons Old Bay seasoning

¼ teaspoon cayenne pepper

→ **After** picking over the crabmeat for cartilage and shell, place the meat in a strainer to get rid of any excess liquid.

Transfer the drained crabmeat to a medium bowl and add the scallions, breadcrumbs, egg, mayonnaise, Old Bay seasoning, and cayenne pepper. Form the crab mixture into 8 patties about ¾ inch thick. Arrange on a platter, cover, and refrigerate for at least 2 hours before grilling.

Prepare enough coals for a medium-hot charcoal fire, or preheat your gas grill on medium-high for 10 minutes with the lid closed.

When the coals are ready or the gas grill is hot, spray the crab cakes liberally with cooking oil. Place on the grate, oiled side down, and grill for 4 minutes. Spray the tops of the cakes, turn, and cook for 4 minutes more, until a nice crust forms and the center is warm.

Transfer immediately to the platter and serve with the chipotle mayonnaise (recipe follows.)

Chipotle Mayonnaise

Quick and easy and packed with flavor, this goes perfectly with the crab cakes.

Makes about ¼ cup

Ingredients

3 tablespoons mayonnaise

2 tablespoons plain yogurt

1 chipotle chile in adobo, seeds removed and finely chopped

2 tablespoons finely chopped scallions, green parts only

1 teaspoon lemon juice

½ teaspoon salt

→ **Mix** all the ingredients together and refrigerate. Let the sauce come to room temperature before serving.

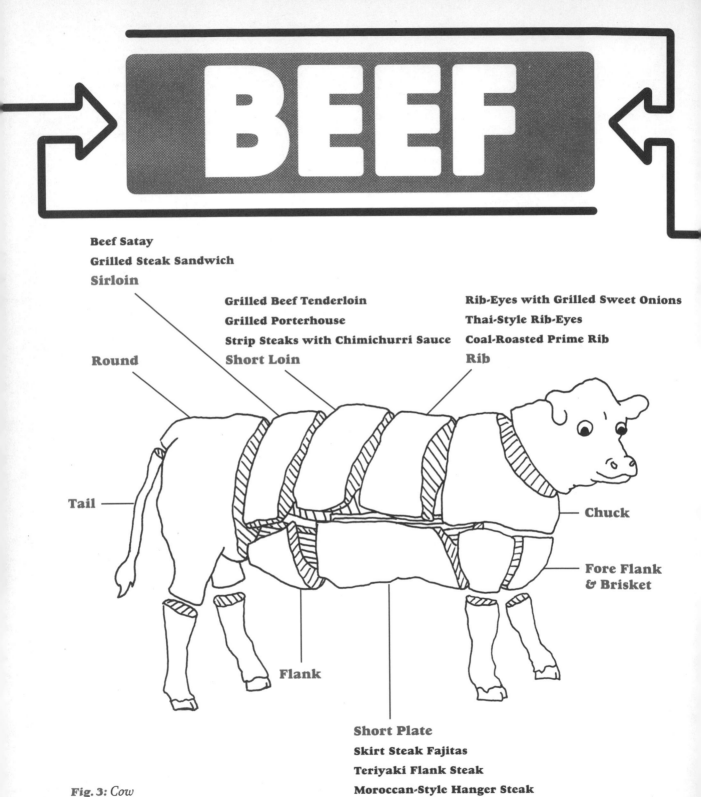

BEEF

Beef Satay
Grilled Steak Sandwich
Sirloin

Grilled Beef Tenderloin
Grilled Porterhouse
Strip Steaks with Chimichurri Sauce
Short Loin

Rib-Eyes with Grilled Sweet Onions
Thai-Style Rib-Eyes
Coal-Roasted Prime Rib
Rib

Round

Tail

Chuck

Fore Flank & Brisket

Flank

Short Plate
Skirt Steak Fajitas
Teriyaki Flank Steak
Moroccan-Style Hanger Steak

Fig. 3: Cow

Few things in life require so little effort and give back so much as a grilled steak. I find it requires more work to cook a steak badly than it does to make it perfect.

Unless The Progeny have become vegetarians, a grill laden with rib-eyes is usually an indication that tonight's dinner is special. It doesn't even require a birthday or a mention on the dean's list or a whole week without a call from the assistant principal. The steaks alone are reason enough to celebrate.

Steak Tips

Here are a few tips to ensure that you grill your steaks to perfection.

1. Let the meat come to room temperature before cooking. This will yield a juicier steak and will allow for a truer cooking time. A half hour at room temperature should do it.

2. Season both sides of your steak with salt just before cooking. There was a nefarious rumor going around for several decades that salting meat before you cook it draws the juices out and makes the steak dry. This is incorrect.

3. Let the meat rest for a few minutes after it's finished cooking before slicing it. I know you've been salivating the whole time your steak was on the grill and can't wait to start carving it up, but please be patient. Letting it rest allows the juices to reincorporate into the fiber of the meat, producing that beautiful roseate center that is so tantalizing.

4. Trim excess fat from the steak before grilling, leaving only about ¼ inch of fat around the edge. Fat shrinks faster than the meat during grilling, and it can cause your steaks to curl. Also, excess fat will cause unwanted flare-ups.

5. Always cook steaks over high heat (except really thick steaks, which require a two-tiered fire). This will sear the meat and get you that great grilled flavor. High heat also produces a juicier steak, though it doesn't actually "seal in the juices" as is sometimes thought.

Dad's Favorite Cuts

New York strip: Lean and flavorful but easy to overcook, so keep an eye on them.

Rib-eyes: Supermarkets usually cut these too thin, so try to get them prepared for you—about $1\frac{1}{2}$ inches thick is best.

Porterhouse: The king of steaks. Just some salt and pepper is all it needs, though I some- times like to serve it with half a lemon, the way they do in Florence.

Flank steak: This cut holds up to a marinade really well. You can let it sit in an Asian- or Southwestern-spiced marinade for up to 24 hours, and it'll just soak up those flavors. After cooking, slice it thinly across the grain.

Skirt steak: If you can find these, they make a great treat on the grill.

Hanger steak: Another cut that will stand up to a potent rub or a marinade.

Steak Glossary

Organic: The cows were fed organic feed— perhaps, but not necessarily, including grass. It does not mean the cows were not given anti- biotics, though organically raised cows are usually not given these medications.

Grass fed: The cows were fed what cows should eat. Grass is a cow's natural food. The meat is flavorful but tends to be leaner.

Natural: An ambiguous designation that may not really mean anything other than that no chemicals were involved in the processing of the meat. Since antibiotics are considered "natural," this label says nothing about whether they were used.

Prime: The highest USDA designation. It implies nothing about the treatment of the cattle, only that the meat has close to perfect marbling, meaning that the fat is distributed within the muscle, making for the most flavorful steak with the ideal juicy texture.

Choice: The next level down from prime, meaning that the fat is less well distributed within the muscle.

Kobe beef: Kobe beef is produced in Japan in limited quantities by traditional methods that are shrouded in mystery. But whether the cattle actually receive regular massages, have their hides rubbed with sake, or drink beer as part of their diet is immaterial once you taste the final product. The meat is perfectly marbled and is exceptionally tender without any shortage of flavor. Domestic Kobe is beginning to become available. Whether it is worth the exorbitant cost is up to you, but if you get some, please let me know.

Aged: Aging beef at the proper temperature allows it to develop a deeper, richer, slightly gamier flavor. Aged beef is more expensive, but when done properly it definitely has more flavor. Whether it's the flavor you want is up to you. The Progeny probably won't be wise to it (but if Dad wants to get one aged steak for himself, that's his prerogative as grill man).

Grilling Times

The times given here are total cooking times—turn your steak halfway through. Also keep in mind that these times are approximate and will vary depending on the heat of your grill, the altitude, and whether your kids are distracting you while you are trying to cook.

Thickness	Rare	Medium-Rare	Medium
1 inch	8 to 10 minutes	10 to 12 minutes	12 to 14 minutes
1½ inches	10 to 12 minutes	12 to 14 minutes	14 to 16 minutes

Internal Temperatures

Beef		Lamb	
Medium-rare	130° to 135°F	Medium-rare	145° to 150°F
Medium	140° to 145°F	Medium	150° to 165°F
Medium-well	150° to 155°F		
Poultry	165° to 175°F	Pork	150°F

Cooking Very Thick Cuts

For steaks more than 1½ inches thick, make a two-level fire—one side hot, one side medium–hot. Start the steaks over the high heat, turning once. Then move them to the medium–hot side, again turning once, to finish cooking. This will allow the outside to become nicely charred but not burned as the inside cooks to the desired doneness.

Rib-Eyes with Grilled Sweet Onions

If there were a magazine devoted to grilling, this would be the centerfold—four sizzling boneless rib-eye steaks framed by thick slices of sweet onions neatly ringing the outer edge of the grill. The hint of chile and cumin works so well with the sweetness of the caramelized onions. You will not need ketchup for these steaks—best inform The Progeny beforehand. **Serves** 4

Ingredients

2 tablespoons salt

1 teaspoon ground cumin

1 teaspoon chili powder

1 teaspoon dried oregano

½ teaspoon cayenne pepper

4 boneless beef rib-eyes,
   cut 1¼ inches thick

3 large sweet onions, peeled and
   cut into ½-inch slices

Spray cooking oil

Salt and freshly ground black pepper

→ **Combine** the salt, cumin, chili powder, oregano, and cayenne in a small bowl and sprinkle evenly over both sides of the steaks.

Prepare enough coals for a two-tiered fire, hot on one side, medium on the other, or preheat your gas grill on high on one side and medium on the other for 10 minutes with the lid closed.

Generously coat both sides of the onion slices with cooking spray, and season to taste with salt and pepper.

When the coals are ready or the gas grill is hot, arrange the onion slices over the medium side of the grill. Place the steaks over the high heat and cook them for 6 minutes, until nicely

browned. Turn and cook for 6 to 7 minutes more, until the steaks are medium-rare.

While the steaks are cooking, turn the onion slices once they are brown on one side, about 5 minutes. When they are completely brown, transfer them to a platter and cover with aluminum foil until the steaks are ready.

Let the steaks rest for 5 minutes before serving, accompanied by the onion slices.

Note: *Thread a short skewer through each slice so it resembles a lollipop—this will help keep the onion intact during grilling.*

Skirt Steak Fajitas

This dish will most definitely impress your kids. First of all, just seeing their dad brazenly wield a cast iron skillet will elevate you to a new Rambo-esque stature. Then when they hear the steak and vegetables furiously sizzling as if at your behest, they will never doubt your toughness again. (Just don't use any pastel potholders.) **Serves** 4

Ingredients

¼ **cup plus 2 tablespoons olive oil**

¼ **cup fresh lime juice**

4 cloves garlic, finely chopped

1 tablespoon chili powder

1 tablespoon ground cumin

1 tablespoon ground coriander

4 skirt steaks (about 1½ pounds total)

1 red onion, thinly sliced

1 red bell pepper, stemmed, seeded, and thinly sliced

¼ **cup chopped fresh cilantro**

1 teaspoon salt

3 limes, 1 cut in half, 2 cut into wedges

8 soft corn or flour tortillas, warmed, for serving

Hot sauce, for serving

→ **In** a small bowl, mix together ¼ cup olive oil, lime juice, garlic, chili powder, cumin, and coriander. Arrange the steaks on a platter and coat with the marinade. Let them sit at room temperature while you get the grill heated up, or cover and refrigerate for up to 4 hours.

Prepare enough coals for a hot charcoal fire, or preheat your gas grill on high for 10 minutes with the lid closed.

When the coals are ready or the gas grill is hot, grill the steaks for 8 to 9 minutes, turning once, until they are medium-rare.

Transfer the steaks to a cutting board and let them rest for 6 minutes, then cut them into thin slices.

While the steaks are resting, place a cast iron or other oven-safe skillet on the grill and let it get hot. Once the meat is sliced, add the remaining 2 tablespoons of olive oil to the skillet and tilt the pan so the oil covers the bottom. Add the onion and bell pepper and cook for 2 minutes. Add the sliced steak along with the cilantro and salt, and mix it all together. Squeeze one of the limes over the mixture and transfer the skillet to the table.

Serve immediately with warm tortillas, hot sauce, and fresh lime wedges, making sure the kids are attentive to the hot pan.

Teriyaki Flank Steak

Once The Progeny get a taste of this, it's sure to become part of the regular dinner rotation. You may even find yourself out in the backyard some winter evening, ankle deep in snow, grilling by flashlight, the tongs gripped tightly in your mittens, the steam from the coals billowing into the cold winter sky. You can remind your kids about this sacrifice years later, in response to their protests after you've grounded them for the weekend to study for midterms. "Hey, who was out there in the middle of winter grilling you your favorite flank steak. Huh?" **Serves 4**

Ingredients

¾ **cup soy sauce**

¼ **cup honey**

2 **teaspoons sesame oil**

2 **cloves garlic, minced**

1 **teaspoon ground ginger**

1 **teaspoon ground cumin**

2 **flank steaks (about 1 pound each)**

Chopped scallions, green parts only, and/or sesame seeds, for garnish

→ **In** a small bowl, stir together the soy sauce, honey, sesame oil, garlic, ginger, and cumin. Spread two-thirds of the marinade on both sides of the flank steaks, and let them sit at room temperature while you get the grill heated up, or refrigerate them in a plastic container for at least 4 hours and up to 24. Reserve the remaining marinade for later.

Prepare enough coals for a very hot charcoal fire, or preheat your gas grill on high for 10 minutes with the lid closed.

When the coals are ready or the gas grill is hot, grill the flank steaks for 10 to 12 minutes, turning once, until medium-rare.

Transfer the steaks to a cutting board and let stand for 6 minutes before slicing thinly across the grain. Arrange the slices on a platter and pour the reserved marinade over them. Garnish with some chopped scallions and/or sesame seeds and serve.

Grilled Beef Tenderloin

The Progeny may have to take on a few extra hours of work-study when they get to college so you can afford this luxurious roast, but it's worth it. The majestic presentation of the whole tenderloin is impressive, and the flavor is killer. But please note: If you are one of those cavalier dads who refuses to consult the directions for even the most complicated assemblies, you have to get over yourself and use the meat thermometer here—too much is at stake. And even if you think it's prissy, it'll be good for The Progeny to see you checking the temperature—it lets them know that, when the situation demands it, even Dad can embrace the right and proper way of doing things. **Serves 8**

Ingredients

1 whole beef tenderloin (about 4 pounds), trimmed

½ cup soy sauce

½ cup red wine

Salt and freshly ground black pepper

¼ cup extra virgin olive oil

Sea salt, for serving

→ **Place** the tenderloin in a bowl or plastic container just large enough to hold it. Add the soy sauce and red wine and let it sit at room temperature while you get the grill heated up.

Prepare enough coals for a two-tiered fire, hot on one side, medium on the other, or preheat your gas grill on high on one side and medium on the other for 10 minutes with the lid closed.

When the coals are ready or the gas grill is hot, remove the tenderloin from the marinade, pat dry, and season well with salt and pepper. Grill the tenderloin over the hot side of the grill for 8 minutes, turning every 2 minutes so it browns evenly.

Transfer to the medium side of the grill and cook for about 12 minutes more, turning regularly, until an instant-read thermometer inserted into the thickest part of the beef registers 130°F for medium-rare.

Transfer the tenderloin to a platter, cover loosely with foil, and let rest for 8 minutes. Present the whole tenderloin at the table, then cut it into 2-inch-thick slices and serve topped with the olive oil, sea salt, and pepper (anything more will detract from the flavor of the meat).

Note: *If you want to add a hint of hickory smoke, at least 1 hour before grilling soak 1 cup of wood chips in water to cover. When the coals are ready, lift the chips from the water and scatter them over the coals. Immediately proceed with the grilling.*

Beef Satay

Thai fish sauce stinks. It smells like locker room, or that bologna sandwich you once left in the glove compartment for the entire second semester of junior year. Despite its malfeasance, make sure The Progeny get a good whiff of it. It will be a great cooking lesson for them. Because once this pungent sauce is balanced with the classic sweet and spicy Thai flavors, it's no longer stinky but part of a perfect flavor combo. This classic dish is well worth the few minutes it takes to throw the marinade together.

Serves 6 to 8

Ingredients

¼ **cup soy sauce**

¼ **cup fresh orange juice**

2 **tablespoons Thai fish sauce**

4 **cloves garlic, finely chopped**

2 **tablespoons fresh lime juice**

2 **tablespoons finely chopped fresh ginger**

2 **tablespoons brown sugar**

1 **tablespoon natural peanut butter**

1 **teaspoon ground cumin**

1 **teaspoon ground coriander**

1 **pound sirloin steak, cut across the grain into ¾-inch-thick strips**

12 **bamboo skewers**

Sliced cucumber and lime wedges, for serving

→ **In** a small bowl, mix together the soy sauce, orange juice, fish sauce, garlic, lime juice, ginger, brown sugar, peanut butter, cumin, and coriander.

Place the steak strips in a large bowl and pour two-thirds of the marinade over them, reserving the remainder. Mix together so all the pieces are coated. Let the steak sit at room temperature while you get the grill heated up, or cover and refrigerate for at least 4 hours and up to 8 hours.

One hour before grilling, soak the bamboo skewers in warm water.

Prepare enough coals for a hot charcoal fire, or preheat your gas grill on high for 10 minutes with the lid closed.

While the coals are heating up, thread 2 strips of steak onto each skewer, keeping them as stretched out as possible. When the coals are ready or the gas grill is hot, grill the steak skewers for 6 to 7 minutes, turning once, until they are just cooked through. Mop with the reserved marinade during the last 2 minutes.

Serve immediately with slices of cucumber and wedges of fresh lime.

Coal-Roasted Prime Rib

They say it's scientifically impossible for bees to fly, and yet they do. It would seem equally improbable that you could cook a 7-pound slab of very expensive meat by laying it on the bottom of your sooty grill and surrounding it with hot coals. Yet it works. The thick shroud of mustard and salt creates a protective crust that keeps in the heat and flavor and keeps out the coal residue. It emerges from the grill's dungeon after two-plus hours like Alec Guinness coming out of solitary in *Bridge on the River Kwai*—grimy but in its full glory. You will need a kettle-style charcoal grill for this dish. Sorry. **Serves 6**

Ingredients

One **3-rib beef roast (7 to 8 pounds)**, trimmed

2 cups Dijon-style mustard

About 2 cups kosher salt

→ **Lay** the roast rib side up on a work surface. Use a rubber spatula to cover the rib side with mustard. Then sprinkle salt over the mustard, pressing it gently to form a crust. Gently turn the roast over and lay it on a wire rack large enough to hold it. Repeat the process with the other side of the roast, using all of the mustard and salt. Let it sit for 20 minutes or so to set while you get the fire started. Add more mustard or salt as needed to keep the coating uniform.

Prepare a large fire in a kettle-style charcoal grill. When the coals are hot, push them to the sides of the grill, making enough space in the center for the roast. Use oven mitts to place the roast, rib side down, among the coals, being careful to disturb the mustard crust as little as possible. Use tongs to arrange the coals so they come right up to the roast.

Cover the grill and cook for about 2 hours and 15 minutes, or until an instant-read meat thermometer registers 135°F for medium-rare, 145°F for medium. Add a handful of coals to the fire every 45 minutes.

Remove the meat to a work surface, cover it with foil, and let it rest for 10 minutes.

Crack off the salt coating and discard, being careful, as it is very hot. Use a brush or paper towel to gently wipe off any remaining salt or ash. You won't get it all, but it just adds to the flavor.

Carve the roast into thick slices. It's best to decide who gets the slices with the bones beforehand.

Thai-Style Rib-Eyes

The Progeny will be quite impressed when Dad makes something that tastes every bit as good as or better than what's served at your local Thai restaurant. **Serves** 4

Ingredients

¼ **cup chopped scallions, green parts only**

6 cloves garlic, coarsely chopped

2 tablespoons vegetable oil

2 tablespoons Thai fish sauce

2 tablespoons brown sugar

1 tablespoon curry powder

4 boneless rib-eye steaks (about 12 ounces each)

Spicy Lime Sauce (recipe on facing page)

Chopped cilantro and/or scallions (green parts only), for garnish

→ **Put** the scallions, garlic, oil, fish sauce, brown sugar, and curry powder in a blender and pulse until smooth. Arrange the steaks on a platter and spread the marinade on both sides. Let them sit at room temperature while the grill is heating up, or cover and refrigerate for at least 4 hours and up to 12 hours.

Prepare enough coals for a hot charcoal fire, or preheat your gas grill on high for 10 minutes with the lid closed.

When the coals are ready or the gas grill is hot, grill the rib-eyes for 8 to 9 minutes, turning once, until medium-rare.

Transfer the steaks to a cutting board and let them sit for 5 minutes before cutting into thin slices. Pour the lime sauce over the sliced meat. Garnish with chopped cilantro and/or scallions and serve.

Spicy Lime Sauce

This sauce features the classic Thai flavor combo of lime, fish sauce, and sugar. **Makes ¾ cup**

Ingredients

½ **cup fresh lime juice**

3 **tablespoons Thai fish sauce**

1 **tablespoon brown sugar**

½ **cup chopped scallions,
  green parts only**

⅓ **cup chopped fresh cilantro**

⅓ **cup chopped fresh mint**

1 **clove garlic, finely chopped**

1 **teaspoon hot sauce**

→ **Mix** all the ingredients together in a small bowl and serve, or cover and refrigerate for up to 48 hours.

Salt & Steak

ONCE THE COALS ARE HOT, it's easy to get caught up in the thrill of the grill and forget one of the simplest and easiest grilling steps—the salt. A liberal sprinkling of kosher salt over the meat before grilling can make all the difference in the outcome. And be sure to distribute the salt evenly over the entire surface. It's not like seasoning a stew, where it diffuses into the mixture during cooking. Always grill the salted side first and then, once the steaks are on the grill, season the tops just before turning.

Grilled Porterhouse

Perhaps the most imposing of steaks, porterhouse requires a bit of finesse to cook. You can't rear back and take a whack at it, as you would with your tee shot on a long par 5. It's more like playing a 100-yard approach shot on a bunker-lined fairway. You may actually have to keep your eyes open when you hit it. You need to make a two-tiered fire—one side hot, the other medium—so you can get the proper char without scorching the meat beyond recognition. The porterhouse actually consists of two different cuts that flank its distinctively large bone. The smaller side is from the tenderloin, the larger side is essentially a strip steak. **Serves** 4

Ingredients

2 porterhouse steaks, about 1½ inches thick (about 3½ pounds total)

Salt and freshly ground black pepper

→ **Season** both sides of the steaks with salt and pepper to taste.

Prepare enough coals for a two-tiered fire, hot on one side, medium on the other, or preheat your gas grill on high on one side and medium on the other for 10 minutes with the lid closed.

When the coals are hot or the grill is ready, cook the steaks on the hot side of the grill for 4 minutes, until they are nicely browned. Turn and grill for 4 minutes more.

Transfer the steaks to the medium side of the grill. Grill for 4 minutes, turn, and grill for about 3 minutes more for medium-rare, about 4 minutes more for medium.

Transfer the steaks to a cutting board and let them rest for 6 minutes. Cut off the strip and tenderloin pieces and slice them each crosswise about ⅓ inch thick.

Serve immediately.

Note: *Each steak will serve 2 people—make sure they each get some of each side.*

Talking to Your Butcher

I AM NOT VERY GOOD at returning things to the store. If they ask me for the receipt and I don't have it, I just walk away. I'm not the guy who has a story ready to tell to cajole or intimidate the salesperson. I'm also not the guy who can discreetly slip a ten-spot to the stadium usher to get those great seats by the field. And though I am getting better at it, I'm still not the guy who can send food back to the kitchen, even when I feel I could go into the kitchen, put on an apron, and cook the dish better.

Despite these foibles, I have no problem talking to a butcher. Any butcher. At the most exclusive gourmet shop or at the local supermarket. The reason for this boldness is that I know the butchers are waiting to talk to me—craving a customer to walk in with a special request, so they don't have to mindlessly throw another pound of chopped meat on the Styrofoam tray and seal it up in the Cryovac. These days, most butchers have been relegated to duties not unlike those of the quarterbacks in the old Ohio State offense—get the snap, hand the ball off to the tailback, and then get out of the way. They are just waiting for a chance to throw one down the field.

Most butchers have mad skills that they are eager to employ, even if they are seemingly stuck behind a generic meat counter at a supermarket. You are doing them a favor by asking for something. So ask. He *knows* the porterhouse steaks he seals up for the meat case are cut too thin. So get him to cut you a couple of thicker ones. He'll be elated. *This* is the way steak should be cut. And if you don't see the skirt steak or short ribs you need, let him know—chances are they can be ordered.

Developing a relationship with a local butcher can save you huge amounts of time. Put him on your speed dial. Call ahead, and he can butterfly a leg of lamb for you, sleeve-bone quail for the whole family, flatten some chicken breasts, or cut pork chops to the thickness you need. You'll both be smiling. He gets a chance to practice his skills, you get some of the prep work done. It's a perfect arrangement.

Moroccan-Style Hanger Steak

I am a big fan of hanger steaks because they play well with others, the "others" in this case being a potent, densely spiced Moroccan-style marinade that might otherwise overwhelm a cut of meat with less fortitude. The Progeny always look forward to this steak coming off the grill, as it's not the typical flavor combo but is still familiar enough for them to totally dig it. Make sure you try it at least once. **Serves 4**

Ingredients

1 medium onion, cut into quarters

½ cup fresh lemon juice

½ cup extra virgin olive oil

¼ cup mint leaves

2 tablespoons finely chopped fresh ginger

2 tablespoons soy sauce

1 tablespoon chili powder

2 teaspoons mild curry powder

2 teaspoons sherry

2 cloves garlic

1 teaspoon freshly ground black pepper

2 pounds hanger steak

➜ **Put** the onion, lemon juice, olive oil, mint, ginger, soy sauce, chili powder, curry powder, sherry, garlic, and black pepper in the container of a food processor or blender and pulse until smooth.

Arrange the hanger steaks on a platter and coat with two-thirds of the marinade, reserving the remainder. Let them sit at room temperature while you get the grill heated up, or cover and refrigerate for up to 4 hours. Prepare enough coals for a hot charcoal fire, or preheat your gas grill on high for 10 minutes with the lid closed.

When the coals are ready or the gas grill is hot, grill the steaks for 8 to 9 minutes, turning once, until they are medium-rare. Mop the steaks on both sides with the reserved marinade during the last 2 minutes of cooking.

Transfer the steaks to a cutting board and let them rest for 5 minutes. Cut them crosswise into slices about ⅓ inch thick.

Serve immediately.

Grilled Steak Sandwich

Why, you may ask, should I go through the trouble of grilling a beautiful piece of sirloin steak only to turn it into a sandwich? Ah, but what a sandwich. This is the zenith *and* the apex of sandwichness. The steak juices start soaking into the bread and it becomes soft and mushy yet is balanced by the crunchy lettuce. The cheese melts divinely and the tangy steak sauce provides just the right enhancement. It's not a sandwich but *memories* you are building here. One day when The Progeny are in college, their *madeleine* will be some sullen, overcooked school cafeteria approximation of a steak sandwich, and their eyes will glaze over and become slightly misty.

"What's wrong, Johnny?"

"Um…I was just thinking back to a steak sandwich my dad used to make for us when we were kids."

"Oh. Wow. Here's a tissue." **Makes 4 sandwiches**

Ingredients

1 teaspoon chili powder

1 teaspoon garlic powder

1 teaspoon dried oregano

1 teaspoon salt

1 teaspoon freshly ground black pepper

2 boneless sirloin steaks, about 1¼ inches thick

2 tablespoons extra virgin olive oil

8 slices country-style white bread

4 slices Colby or Monterey Jack cheese

4 nice leaves romaine lettuce

Steak sauce, for serving

→ **In** a small bowl, combine the chili powder, garlic powder, oregano, salt, and pepper. Brush both sides of the steak with olive oil and season with the spice mixture.

Prepare enough coals for a hot charcoal fire, or preheat your gas grill on high for 10 minutes with the lid closed.

When the coals are ready or the gas grill is hot, grill the steaks for 9 to 10 minutes, turning once, until they are medium-rare.

Transfer the steaks to a cutting board and let them rest for 6 minutes. Cut them crosswise into slices about ⅓ inch thick. Divide the steak slices among 4 slices of the bread. Top with a slice of cheese and a leaf of romaine. Serve immediately, with steak sauce on the side.

Strip Steaks with Chimichurri Sauce

Argentineans like to eat a lot of beef. And a lot of the beef they eat is accompanied by this garlicky, citrus-infused sauce that instantly perks up whatever you use it on. If you make the sauce ahead of time, be sure to take it out of the fridge at least 30 minutes beforehand so you can serve it at room temperature. **Serves** 4

Ingredients

1 cup packed fresh parsley leaves

1 cup packed fresh mint leaves

⅓ cup extra virgin olive oil

¼ cup fresh lemon juice

5 cloves garlic, mashed

½ teaspoon ground cumin

½ teaspoon red pepper flakes

½ teaspoon dried oregano

1 teaspoon salt, plus more for seasoning steak

4 boneless strip steaks, cut 1¼ inches thick

Freshly ground black pepper

→ **Place** the parsley, mint, olive oil, lemon juice, garlic, cumin, pepper flakes, oregano, and 1 teaspoon of the salt in the bowl of a food processor fitted with a steel blade, and pulse until smooth. Set aside until ready to use. The sauce can be kept for up to 2 days in the refrigerator, in a well-sealed container with a piece of plastic wrap laid directly over the surface of the sauce.

Prepare enough coals for a hot charcoal fire, or preheat your gas grill on high for 10 minutes with the lid closed.

When the coals are ready or the gas grill is hot, season the steaks with salt and pepper and grill them for 9 to 10 minutes, turning once, until they are medium-rare.

Transfer the steaks to a platter and let them rest for 5 minutes. Serve immediately, with the *chimichurri* sauce on the side.

Teaching Your Kids to Cook

TEACHING MY SON TO SHAVE was easy. One Saturday morning, while I stood in front of the bathroom mirror still foggy from the shower, my son came in, sat down on the closed toilet seat, and settled in to watch me shave. Like my dad, I use a shaving brush, and as I was lathering up, somehow the brush slipped and wound up tickling my son's cheek. There was laughter, then retaliation, threats of yanking off my towel.

But as I took out my razor and started to shave he quieted down, listening intently as I described the proper angle for the blade, the different directions to pull it in, the tricky maneuvers around my chin. This was serious business, as he knew that some day he, too, would be standing there before the mirror, razor in hand.

I have tried to initiate the same kind of process in the kitchen. I operate under the assumption that some day my son will be will be wielding a spatula as well as a razor—cooking for himself or friends or family. I keep the instructions simple in the kitchen. I let him watch as I work, taking in my enthusiasm and attention to detail. I explain as I go, making it clear that for me cooking is not about being fancy or pretentious, it's about self-reliance. Just as you wouldn't expect someone to shave you, you shouldn't expect someone to cook for you.

But unlike shaving, for my son there is still a lingering stigma against men being in the kitchen for anything other than grabbing a beer and a bag of chips. Dad and son working together in the kitchen is not the typical image of fathers and sons playing. It's not like catch in the backyard, trout fishing, or flying a kite. (But have you ever actually been able to get a kite in the air? Because I think that happens only in the movies, after the Teamsters kite-flying guy has gotten it airborne—and even *he* had a hard time.) Nevertheless, my son and I do a fair amount of cooking together, especially at the grill. We stand shoulder to shoulder, each with a pair of tongs, watching the proceedings carefully. Indeed, cooking together has been some of the more harmonious time we've spent in each other's company. It was far more tranquil, for instance, than the parallel parking process that resulted in a block-long line of cars blaring their horns at us while we tried to resolve our differing interpretations of just how and when the wheel should be cut.

It's always important not to underestimate what The Progeny can do. If they want to get involved, don't offer them only the mundane chores, what they call the "dog's work" in France, and save the fun stuff for yourself. You're not a three-star chef and they're not your apprentices. If they can stir or mix, they can also chop and slice and add the seasoning.

In this way, unlike, say, doing the laundry (or, for that matter, identifying which of the clothes festooned about The Progeny's room *are* laundry), cooking will hopefully not seem like a chore.

Try to let the rhythm of the food take over. Once they begin to feel what so many chefs experience, that cooking is relaxing and—dare I say it?—fun, they will only want to do more. It may sound maudlin, but cooking is a lot like childhood—just a series of transformations—from whole to chopped, from uncooked to cooked, from less flavor to more flavor, from uninviting to (hopefully) appealing. Let them get a sense of the *before* and *after* for each of these processes and they will be on their way to being able to cook anything they want.

Veal Chops with Morels

This dish is for that special summer Saturday evening when the Two of You are alone. Perhaps The Progeny are off to camp or on some weeklong educational escapade, or maybe earlier in the day you stopped by your in-laws' place unannounced and dropped them there for an overnight, which, tomorrow, you will extend for a few days because, after all, what are your in-laws going to do—toss their grandkids out on the street? So anyway, by hook or by crook, the Two of You are alone for the night and this is what you want to make. The earthy flavor of the morels, bathed in the Marsala-infused sauce, is just the right way to kick off a special evening. Serve with some Walter Hensel Pinot from California. If your wine shop doesn't have it, say you want something just as good. If they have never heard of it, find another wine shop.

Serves 2

Ingredients

2 ounces dried morel mushrooms

2 cups warm water

2 slices thick-cut bacon, cut crosswise
   into ¼-inch strips

1 medium onion, finely chopped

2 cloves garlic, finely chopped

¼ cup Marsala wine (see Note)

½ cup canned unsalted chicken broth

½ cup heavy cream

¼ cup chopped fresh basil

Salt and freshly ground black pepper

2 veal loin chops (about 12 ounces each)

2 tablespoons extra virgin olive oil

→ **Soak** the morels in the warm water for 1 hour. When they've reconstituted, lift each mushroom and examine the folds to see if any grit has stuck there. If you find any, gently brush it off. Only if there is a lot of grit should you rinse them. Cut each mushroom in half lengthwise and set aside. Save the soaking liquid.

Place a large, heavy skillet over medium-high heat. Add the bacon and cook, stirring regularly, until it is just crisp, about 5 minutes. Using a slotted spoon, transfer the bacon to a plate lined with paper towels and set aside.

Reduce the heat to medium-low and pour out all but 1 tablespoon of the bacon fat. Add the onions and cook until they are soft, about 7 minutes. Add the mushrooms and garlic and cook, stirring frequently, for 2 more minutes.

Increase the heat to high and return the bacon to the pan. Add the Marsala and cook, stirring frequently, until the liquid has reduced by half. Add the chicken broth, 2 tablespoons of the morel soaking liquid, and the cream. When the liquid comes to a simmer, reduce the heat to low and cook, stirring continuously, until the sauce thickens and is reduced by half, about 5 minutes. Add the basil, reserving 1 tablespoon for garnishing, and season to taste with salt and pepper. The sauce can be made up to 1 day in advance. Add a few tablespoons of broth or cream when reheating.

Prepare enough coals for a hot charcoal fire, or preheat your gas grill on high for 10 minutes with the lid closed.

While the coals are heating up, brush the chops on both sides with the olive oil and season to taste with salt and pepper.

When the coals are ready or the gas grill is hot, grill the veal chops for 8 to 9 minutes, turning once, until just medium.

Transfer each veal chop to a dinner plate. Pour half the sauce over each chop, garnish with the remaining basil, and, goshdarnit, serve them already!

Note: *If you don't have any Marsala on hand, you can use some dry white vermouth or a fruity white wine.*

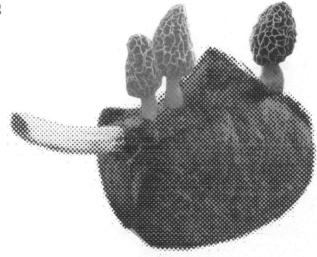

PORK

Cherries: barbeque sauce's best friend

Slightly left of center cut

Center cut

Fig. 4: Pork Chops with Cherry Barbecue Sauce

Pork just belongs on the barbecue. The fattier cuts, like the ribs and shoulder, settle in for a long, slow, comfy spell on the grill, much as your brother-in-law does on the rec-room divan during the holidays.

The longer and slower they cook, the more they soak up the smoke and flavor. Leaner cuts are enhanced over high heat, picking up the flavor of the coals or fire, developing a lovely charred outside and a juicy, succulent center. Pork lends itself to intense, almost indecent marinades. It also usually does well with some attentive mopping during the last few minutes on the grill.

Some of the best cuts for grilling are not the ones most commonly found packaged in the supermarket meat case. The chops are usually too thin, for example. And the Boston butt you find will probably have been cut into sections. This means you may have to open a dialogue with your butcher, something every self-respecting, grill-wise dad should do (see page 47).

Honey-Glazed Spareribs

The name says it all. Besides their succulence, their infectious flavor, and their being part of one big joyful and fabulously tasty and messy meal, these ribs are the perfect starting place for your kids to practice their grilling. Because you precook the ribs, and therefore they require only a short time on the grill, you can set up The Progeny with a pair of tongs and a grill brush and let them go to work. Also, the flavor of these ribs is so pronounced that it is very hard to screw them up, even for a grill novice. Get a gold star—or better yet, wrap up a new pair of tongs in a red ribbon—and present them to each assistant at dinner in honor of the occasion. **Serves** 4

Ingredients

½ **cup white wine**

½ **cup soy sauce**

1 **bunch scallions, green parts only, finely chopped**

3 **tablespoons finely chopped fresh ginger**

8 **cloves garlic, coarsely chopped**

6 **tablespoons brown sugar**

1 **tablespoon Chinese five-spice powder**

Pinch ground cayenne pepper

3 **to 4 pounds spareribs (about 2 slabs), cut into individual ribs**

Honey Glaze (recipe on facing page)

→ **Preheat** the oven to 350°F.

In a large bowl, combine the wine, soy sauce, scallions, ginger, garlic, brown sugar, five-spice powder, and cayenne.

Place the ribs in the bowl with the wine mixture, tossing them gently so they are all coated evenly. Transfer the ribs and liquid to a baking pan, cover with foil, and bake in the center of the oven for 1 hour. Let the ribs cool, then transfer them to a plastic container and refrigerate for up to 2 days.

To finish the ribs on the grill, prepare enough coals for a medium-hot charcoal fire, or preheat your gas grill on medium-high for 10 minutes with the lid closed.

When the coals are ready or the gas grill is hot, grill the ribs until they are heated through, about 15 minutes, turning and mopping them several times with the Honey Glaze so they are nicely coated.

Serve immediately with lots of napkins.

Honey Glaze

A delectable sweet and spicy finish for spareribs. Feel free to use it with chicken or pork dishes if the right occasion arises. **Makes about 2 cups**

Ingredients

⅔ **cup honey**

½ **cup fresh orange juice**

¼ **cup fresh lemon juice**

3 **tablespoons soy sauce**

2 **tablespoons Dijon-style mustard**

1 **tablespoon sesame oil**

1 **teaspoon curry powder**

1 **teaspoon ground ginger**

➔ **In** a medium bowl, stir together the honey, orange juice, lemon juice, soy sauce, mustard, sesame oil, curry powder, and ginger. Set aside until ready to use, or refrigerate, covered, for up to 1 week. Let the glaze come to room temperature before using.

Beer-Besotted Slow-Cooked Pork Loin

Before The Progeny make any crude remarks, assure them that marinating pork (and chicken) in beer before grilling is a time–honored barbecue tradition and not something you invented on one of those Sunday afternoons when you disappeared into the garage "to work on the car" and didn't come out until several hours later with no sign of grease on your hands. The beer lends flavor and texture to the pork, though no one is exactly sure why. Rest assured, however, that as with all additions of wine and liquor in these recipes, the alcohol cooks off during grilling. **Serves** 4

Ingredients

One **12-ounce can beer**

½ **cup brown sugar**

½ **cup finely chopped onion**

¼ **cup vegetable oil**

2 **tablespoons Dijon-style mustard**

1 **tablespoon chili powder**

1 **teaspoon garlic powder**

½ **teaspoon ground allspice**

3 **pounds boneless pork loin**

→ **In** a small bowl, combine the beer, brown sugar, onion, oil, mustard, chili powder, garlic powder, and allspice and mix together. Place the pork loin in a large, shallow dish. Pour the marinade over the pork, cover, and refrigerate for at least 4 hours and up to 12 hours, turning the loin halfway through.

Prepare enough coals for a medium charcoal fire, or preheat one side of your gas grill on medium for 10 minutes with the lid closed.

When the coals are ready or the gas grill is hot, pile the coals on one side of the coal grate. Place a drip pan on the other side. Place the pork loin on the grill grate directly over the drip pan or on the side away from the heat on a gas grill. Cover the grill and slow–cook the loin for about 1 hour and 15 minutes, or until a meat thermometer reads 150°F. Let the loin rest for 6 minutes before slicing.

Back Seat Secrets

APPARENTLY, when he was in seventh grade, my son was walking down the aisle of the school bus when he accidentally tripped over a backpack and landed on another kid. This other boy was known around school for being somewhat tough, and he was not pleased when my son landed in his lap. He proceeded to take umbrage at the intrusion and threatened to do him bodily harm. The Boy challenged him, brazenly saying he'd take the kid on any time. They then stared at each other, not saying anything, until The Boy turned away and walked to his seat.

I know the details of this not insignificant event in my son's life not because he told me, not because we had any kind of serious father/son chat (though not for lack of trying on my part), but because I had to drive him and two of his friends to a party one night. The three boys sat in the back seat and talked nonstop the entire way there and back. They spoke without censure, as if there were a soundproof barrier between the front and back seats. They recounted the bus incident, mused about their teachers, gossiped about budding romances, how badly each was doing in Spanish, and what they thought about certain movies (movies we saw *together*, movies I thought he *liked*).

I confess that driving my son and his friends has become my principal means of obtaining the inside dope on a great number of important events in my son's life. No matter how many times it hap-pens, it still strikes me as a remarkably curious phenomenon—the ability for me, Dad, to completely disappear in the front seat. Details I've tried in vain to cajole from him spill forth with ease and candor when he's in the back seat. It almost feels like cheating. On this one ride I not only got the lowdown on the thug incident on the bus, but also on how he performed on a recent test, what book he's reading, and how he's doing in Spanish.

Now it's not as though I'm uninvolved. I'm totally there, eagerly plying him like Mata Hari for information, for what's new, how things are going. At dinner we all chat together, my wife and I letting the conversation flow, hoping it might drift toward what's going on in his life. But we manage only to obtain snippets of information couched in gentle tones, purposefully packaged so as not to get us riled. We get sound bites, with spin worthy of the most seasoned politico.

Seventh graders apparently still believe that loose lips sink ships. So while other parents balk, I now jump at the chance to be the driver, eager to get the inside scoop, the skinny from the back seat.

Spicy Pork & Pineapple Kabobs

I have a special affinity for pork and pineapple. When I was a kid, my mom would occasionally try to make a Real Gourmet Meal. One of these featured a garish and disconcertingly pink canned ham with a Gumby-like texture that looked as though it had been beamed into our kitchen from some futuristic Jetson-style food portal. To its impossibly sleek triangular shape she affixed bright yellow pineapple rings, each one's center adorned with a lurid red maraschino cherry. This wasn't everyday food. To my Mom, it spoke of a world of grace and elegance far beyond our banal and predictable suburban kitchen. It was the domain of effete gourmands—large men from indeterminable European countries sporting thin mustaches who knew about *real* cooking, the *gourmet* kind. The Progeny happen to love these kabobs, but as soon as they release a DVD box set of *Mannix* or *Daktari* I'm going to prepare for them one of those pink, pineapple-ringed Technicolor hams. But do they even make maraschino cherries anymore? **Serves 4**

Ingredients

¼ **cup vegetable oil**

2 **scallions, green parts only, coarsely chopped**

2 **cloves garlic, coarsely chopped**

¼ **cup honey**

3 **tablespoons soy sauce**

2 **tablespoons fresh lime juice**

1 **tablespoon curry powder**

1½ **pounds pork tenderloin, cut into 1-inch pieces**

8 **bamboo skewers**

Twelve **1-inch pieces fresh pineapple, or one 8-ounce can pineapple chunks, drained**

1 **red bell pepper, stemmed, seeded, and cut into ¾-inch pieces**

Spray cooking oil

Peanut-Coconut Sauce (recipe on facing page), for serving

→ **Place** the vegetable oil, scallions, garlic, honey, soy sauce, lime juice, and curry powder in the container of a food processor or blender and pulse until well combined. Transfer to a plastic container and add the pork pieces. Let marinate for 1 hour at room temperature or for up to 12 hours in the refrigerator.

One hour before grilling, soak the bamboo skewers in warm water.

Prepare enough coals for a hot charcoal fire, or preheat your gas grill on high for 10 minutes with the lid closed.

While the coals are heating up, thread the pork, pineapple, and red pepper onto the skewers, making sure not to crowd them too closely.

When the coals are ready or the gas grill is hot, spray the kabobs with oil on all sides and grill them for about 10 minutes, turning every 2 minutes or so, until all sides are cooked equally and the pork is just cooked through.

Transfer the kabobs to a serving platter and serve immediately with the peanut sauce.

Peanut-Coconut Sauce

Everything tastes better with this sauce. If you need a quick appetizer, cut up some red peppers, cucumbers, and carrots and serve them with a bowl of peanut sauce. You may not even need a main course. **Makes about 1 cup**

Ingredients

½ **cup unsweetened coconut milk**
¼ **cup natural peanut butter**
1 **clove garlic, finely chopped**
1 **tablespoon fresh lime juice**
2 **teaspoons soy sauce**
2 **teaspoons Thai fish sauce**
1 **teaspoon brown sugar**

→ **Place** all the ingredients in the container of a food processor or blender and pulse until mixed together. Set aside until ready to use, or cover and refrigerate for up to 24 hours.

Pork Chops with Cherry Barbecue Sauce

We spend our summers in a quiet corner of northwest Lower Michigan, which, after Washington State, is the country's largest cherry producer. The counties in our area are covered with cherry trees, and in early July, during the harvest, the sides of the road are dappled crimson from stray fruit that has fallen from the trucks on the way to the processing plant. We use cherries in everything, including the slightly sweet and pungent barbecue sauce that is doused over these chops. **Serves** 4

Ingredients

½ **cup fresh orange juice**

2 **tablespoons extra virgin olive oil**

1 **tablespoon brown sugar**

1 **tablespoon chili powder**

1 **teaspoon ground cumin**

4 **boneless pork loin chops, cut 1 inch thick**

Cherry Barbecue Sauce (recipe on facing page)

→ **Combine** the orange juice, olive oil, brown sugar, chili powder, and cumin in a small bowl and stir together.

Spread the marinade on both sides of the pork chops and let them sit at room temperature for 30 minutes, or refrigerate them in a plastic container for up to 12 hours.

Prepare enough coals for a medium–hot charcoal fire, or preheat your gas grill on medium–high for 10 minutes with the lid closed.

When the coals are ready or the gas grill is hot, grill the pork chops for 8 to 9 minutes, turning once, until they are just cooked through. Mop the chops on both sides with some of the Cherry Barbecue Sauce during the last 2 minutes of cooking.

Transfer to a serving platter and serve immediately with more of the Cherry Barbecue Sauce.

Cherry Barbecue Sauce

The cherries work surprisingly well to add just the right touch of sweetness to this sauce. **Makes about 2 cups**

Ingredients

1 tablespoon vegetable oil

1 medium onion, finely chopped

3 cloves garlic, finely chopped

1 tablespoon chili powder

3 tablespoons tomato paste

1½ cups water

½ cup fresh orange juice

¼ cup ketchup

¼ cup light brown sugar

1 cup pitted sweet cherries, thawed if frozen

½ teaspoon salt

→ **Place** a medium saucepan over medium-high heat. When the pan gets hot, add the oil and the onion and cook until the onion softens, about 6 minutes. Add the garlic and chili powder and cook for 1 minute more. Add the tomato paste, water, orange juice, ketchup, brown sugar, cherries, and salt and simmer for 10 minutes longer, stirring regularly.

Let the sauce cool, then transfer it to a plastic container and refrigerate until ready to serve, or for up to 1 week.

Cider & Honey-Glazed Pork Chops

One reason The Progeny like these pork chops so much is that whenever they are on the menu they are accompanied by Dad's Pear–Apple–Cranberry Crisp (see page 213). Served in tandem, they become the perfect autumn meal. **Serves** 4

Ingredients

1½ cups apple cider

2 tablespoons honey

2 tablespoons soy sauce

2 tablespoons fresh lemon juice

½ teaspoon dried sage

½ teaspoon ground ginger

Pinch freshly grated nutmeg

4 boneless pork loin chops,
    cut 1 inch thick

Salt and freshly ground black pepper

Chopped scallions, green parts only,
    for garnish

→ **Combine** the cider, honey, soy sauce, lemon juice, sage, ginger, and nutmeg in a small saucepan and simmer until thick and syrupy, 3 to 5 minutes.

Prepare enough coals for a medium-hot charcoal fire, or preheat your gas grill on medium-high for 10 minutes with the lid closed. While the coals are heating, season the pork chops on both sides with salt and pepper to taste.

When the coals are ready or the gas grill is hot, grill the pork chops for 8 to 9 minutes, turning once, until they are just cooked through.

Transfer the chops to a platter and pour the cider glaze over them. Serve garnished with a few tablespoons of chopped scallions.

Pork Chops Asado

You have probably walked past asado paste a thousand times in the supermarket, assuming you've been to the supermarket a thousand times. It sits in the international section, which is the area of the supermarket you should be most familiar with. After all, the capitals of Europe sent out their explorers in search not of meat or dairy, but of spices. Asado is a combination of chile peppers, garlic, and spices that instantly turns these pork chops into something spectacular. **Serves** 4

Ingredients

½ **cup fresh orange juice**

¼ **cup fresh lemon juice**

2 **tablespoons vegetable oil**

2 **tablespoons apple cider vinegar**

2 **cloves garlic, crushed**

4 **boneless pork chops, cut about 1 inch thick**

2 **tablespoons asado paste**

→ **In** a large bowl, combine the orange juice, lemon juice, oil, vinegar, and garlic. Rub both sides of the chops with asado and transfer them to the bowl with the orange juice mixture, making sure the chops are covered completely. Let them sit at room temperature for 30 minutes, or cover and refrigerate for at least 1 hour and up to 12 hours.

Prepare enough coals for a medium charcoal fire, or preheat your gas grill on medium for 10 minutes with the lid closed.

When the coals are ready or the gas grill is hot, remove the chops from the marinade and grill them for 8 to 9 minutes, turning once, until they are just cooked through. Transfer to a platter and serve immediately.

Jerk Pork Tenderloin

Making truly authentic jerk pork is a tricky proposition. Most family recipes are closely guarded secrets, and fake recipes are often given to the public as a distraction, much as truffle hunters dig at the bottom of trees where no truffles are so other hunters will waste time at that spot the following year. But this recipe comes pretty close to what you might find at a roadside stand in Jamaica, where the best jerk food is served. That said, even a casual jerk fan will immediately notice the glaring omission of Scotch bonnet peppers from the recipe. Though essential to most true jerk recipes, they are so hot I feel it would unwise for Dad to employ them. Despite that, this pork tenderloin will have you playing some Dennis Brown during dinner. **Serves 4**

Ingredients

1 small onion, coarsely chopped

1 cup coarsely chopped scallions, green parts only

1 tablespoon finely chopped fresh ginger

1 tablespoon fresh lime juice

1 tablespoon soy sauce

1 tablespoon Worcestershire sauce

1 tablespoon vegetable oil

1 tablespoon dark rum

2 teaspoons fresh thyme, or 1 teaspoon dried

2 teaspoons brown sugar

1 teaspoon salt

½ teaspoon ground allspice

½ teaspoon freshly grated nutmeg

2 pork tenderloins (about 1 pound each)

Spray cooking oil

→ **Combine** the onion, scallions, ginger, lime juice, soy sauce, Worcestershire sauce, oil, rum, thyme, brown sugar, salt, allspice, and nutmeg in the container of a food processor or blender, and pulse until the mixture is smooth.

Butterfly the tenderloins by cutting them horizontally through the center almost to the end and then opening the meat up like a book. The meat should lie flat.

Place the pork in a shallow dish. Spread the marinade on both sides of the tenderloins and refrigerate in a plastic container for at least 4 hours and up to 24 hours. The longer it sits, the more profound the jerk flavor.

Prepare enough coals for a medium-hot charcoal fire, or preheat your gas grill on medium-high for 10 minutes with the lid closed.

Spray the tenderloins liberally with oil and place them oiled side down on the grill grate. Grill for 7 minutes. Spray the tops with oil, turn, and cook for 6 to 7 minutes more, until the thickest part is just cooked through.

Transfer the tenderloins to a cutting board and let rest for 6 minutes. Cut into thin slices and serve.

Grilled Pork Steak

The pork steak is an unheralded cut that comes alive with fearless seasoning and some exposure to a hot grill. This is a manly piece of meat, like something a rancher might eat after a long day riding his spread. The precut pork steaks available at most supermarkets will likely be too thin for this recipe. Instead, order a blade roast and have it sliced about ¾ inch thick. You can make the Smoky Barbecue Sauce from the recipe included here or serve it with your favorite bottled sauce. **Serves** 4

Ingredients

¼ **cup paprika**

3 **tablespoons chili powder**

2½ **tablespoons dry mustard**

2 **tablespoons salt**

2 **tablespoons sugar**

2 **tablespoons ground cumin**

2 **tablespoons granulated garlic**

½ **teaspoon cayenne pepper**

4 **pork steaks, cut ¾ inch thick (about 14 ounces each)**

Smoky Barbecue Sauce (recipe on facing page)

→ **Combine** the paprika, chili powder, dry mustard, salt, sugar, cumin, garlic, and cayenne in a small bowl and stir together.

Spread the rub liberally on both sides of the pork steaks and let them sit at room temperature for 30 minutes, or refrigerate them in a plastic container for at least 4 hours and up to 24 hours.

Prepare enough coals for a medium-hot charcoal fire, or preheat your gas grill on medium-high for 10 minutes with the lid closed.

When the coals are ready or the gas grill is hot, grill the pork steaks for 10 to 12 minutes, turning once, until they are just cooked through. Mop the pork steaks on both sides with some barbecue sauce during the last 2 minutes of cooking.

Transfer to a serving platter and serve immediately with more of the barbecue sauce.

Smoky Barbecue Sauce

The bacon and tart apple conspire to give this sauce a unique pungence. It's not really authentic to anywhere, so feel free to ascribe it a pedigree of your own devising. Or just say it's from your hometown. **Makes about 1½ cups**

Ingredients

3 slices thick-cut bacon, finely chopped

1 medium onion, finely chopped

½ tart apple, peeled, cored, and finely chopped

3 cloves garlic, finely chopped

1 cup ketchup

¼ cup apple cider vinegar

¼ cup apple juice

½ cup brown sugar

2 tablespoons Worcestershire sauce

1 tablespoon Dijon-style mustard

¼ teaspoon cayenne pepper

→ **Heat** a large saucepan over medium-low heat. Add the bacon and cook until golden brown, about 4 minutes. Add the onion, apple, and garlic and cook for 4 minutes more. Add the ketchup, vinegar, apple juice, brown sugar, Worcestershire sauce, mustard, and cayenne and simmer, stirring often, until the sauce begins to thicken, about 10 minutes.

Let cool and transfer to a plastic container. Cover and refrigerate for up to 1 week.

Rolled Pork Shoulder

This is a good dish to have in your arsenal because you can make it in advance, up to two days before you want to serve it. Then all you need to do is slice it and reheat it on the grill. It makes a perfect entrée to serve when you're hosting a small party of, say, eight people, as you won't have to be frantically preparing the main course when your guests arrive, allowing you to schmooze at your leisure. (Though with certain guests, having a reason to stay sequestered by the grill is probably a good thing.) The earthy flavor of the sauce and the dramatic presentation make this a meal for special occasions.
Serves 8

Ingredients

Pork shoulder or leg (about 3 pounds), butterflied and pounded to yield 1 large piece, about 1½ inches thick and 12 inches square (ask your butcher to do this for you)

Kosher salt and freshly ground black pepper

1 bunch Italian parsley, finely chopped

½ cup pine nuts

½ cup dried currants

½ cup freshly grated Parmigiano-Reggiano cheese, plus more for garnish

16 slices prosciutto (about 5 ounces)

Several gratings of nutmeg

¼ cup dried oregano

¼ cup extra virgin olive oil

2 red onions, finely chopped

4 cloves garlic, thinly sliced

2 cups dry white wine

Two 28-ounce cans crushed Italian tomatoes with juice

2 teaspoons red pepper flakes

→ **Lay** the pork on a cutting board and lightly season with salt and pepper.

In a mixing bowl, stir together the parsley (reserve a couple of tablespoons for garnish), pine nuts, currants, and Parmigiano-Reggiano and season with salt and pepper.

Lay the prosciutto slices over the pork to cover it completely. Sprinkle the parsley mixture evenly over the prosciutto. Grate nutmeg over everything and sprinkle with 2 tablespoons of the oregano.

Carefully roll the pork up like a jelly roll and tie it firmly with butcher's twine in several places. Season the roll with salt and pepper. The meat may be refrigerated for a day or two at this point.

Place an 8-quart Dutch oven over high heat, add the oil, and heat until smoking. Carefully brown the pork roll on all sides, taking your time to get a deep golden brown; this should take 10 to 15 minutes. Remove the meat and set aside.

Lower the heat slightly, add the onions, the remaining 2 tablespoons oregano, and the garlic to the pan and cook until lightly browned and soft, about 8 minutes.

Add the wine, tomatoes, and pepper flakes and bring to a boil. Return the pork to the pan and simmer, with the pan covered, for 1 hour and 20 minutes. Let the pork cool in the liquid, then refrigerate for up to 24 hours.

When you are ready to serve, prepare enough coals for a medium-hot charcoal fire, or preheat your gas grill on medium-high for 10 minutes with the lid closed.

While the grill is heating, remove the pork from the sauce and slice it on a slight angle into $1\frac{1}{2}$-inch slices. Place the pan with the sauce on the stove over low heat.

When the coals are ready or the gas grill is hot, grill the pork slices for 5 to 6 minutes, turning once, until they are heated through.

Transfer the pork to a serving platter and top with the heated sauce. Serve garnished with grated Parmigiano-Reggiano and the reserved chopped parsley.

LAMB

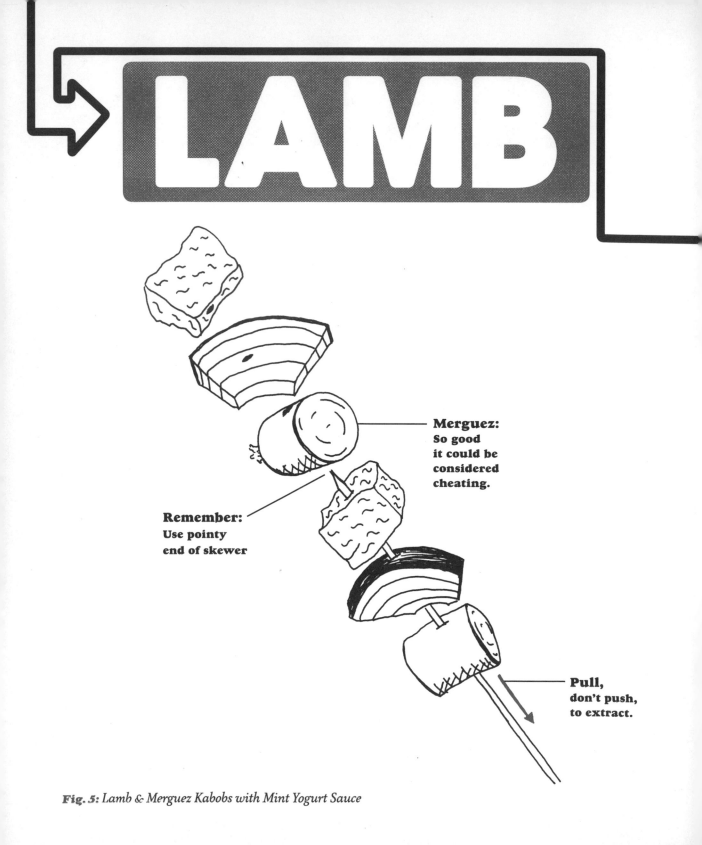

Merguez:
So good
it could be
considered
cheating.

Remember:
Use pointy
end of skewer

Pull,
don't push,
to extract.

Fig. 5: *Lamb & Merguez Kabobs with Mint Yogurt Sauce*

05

For me, lamb is made for the grill. In winter, I'll cook up a lamb stew once in a while, but usually I wait until it starts getting warm so I can prepare my lamb the way I like it, on the grill.

Of the different cuts, the leg is my favorite. I have the butcher take out the bone and butterfly it for me. All I have to do then is whip together the marinade, build the fire, and throw it on the grill.

I like to serve grilled lamb medium-rare, but it has to be a true medium-rare. That means it has a touch of pink in the center, but nothing that is uncooked. Unlike beef, the texture of rare lamb is not very inviting. The Progeny prefer their lamb more in the medium range. With the grilled whole leg it's easy enough to find some pieces around the ends that are more well-done and also have enough from the center that's medium-rare.

Lamb takes well to marinades, especially those with lots of garlic. After it's cooked, you can try serving it with the traditional mint jelly, though I'm inclined to the less familiar condiments. The main thing is to be brave with lamb. The cuts don't look like steaks—they're sometimes not of a uniform thickness or a neat shape. Just trust that the heat of the grill will do the work for you, though you may have to make some executive decisions about leaving the thicker pieces on the grill so they can cook for a few minutes longer.

Lamb Picadillo

The combination of olives, currants, and spices makes this Mexican sauce one of The Progeny's favorites. Sometimes we prepare it on the stove in the more traditional manner with ground beef or turkey and use it as a filling for tacos. But I especially like employing *picadillo* in this guise, poured over freshly grilled lamb kabobs. This is one of those dishes that requires a bit of work in the kitchen before you get out to the grill, but once you add *picadillo* to your repertoire, you'll be looking for any excuse to prepare it. **Serves** 4

Ingredients

1 tablespoon vegetable oil

1 medium onion, finely chopped

3 cloves garlic, finely chopped

1 tablespoon chili powder

1 teaspoon ground coriander

1 teaspoon ground cumin

1 teaspoon dried oregano

½ teaspoon ground cinnamon

¼ teaspoon ground cloves

⅓ cup chicken broth

One 12-ounce can crushed tomatoes

½ cup coarsely chopped green olives

¼ cup dried currants

8 bamboo skewers

1½ pounds boneless lamb from the leg or shoulder, cut into 1-inch cubes

Salt and freshly ground black pepper

Chopped scallions and/or parsley, for garnish

→ **Place** a medium, heavy-bottomed saucepan over medium-high heat. When the pan gets hot, add the oil and then the onion and cook, stirring regularly, until it softens, about 7 minutes. Add the garlic, chili powder, coriander, cumin, oregano, cinnamon, and cloves and cook for 1 minute more, stirring constantly.

Add the chicken broth and cook until it is reduced by half, about 2 minutes. Add the tomatoes, olives, and currants and bring the mixture to a boil. Immediately reduce the heat to low and simmer, uncovered, for 6 minutes. Let the mixture cool in the skillet and set aside, or transfer to a plastic container and refrigerate for up to 2 days.

One hour before grilling, soak the skewers in warm water.

Prepare enough coals for a medium-hot charcoal fire, or preheat your gas grill on medium-high for 10 minutes with the lid closed.

While the coals are heating up, thread the lamb pieces onto the skewers, making sure not to crowd them too closely. Season on all sides with salt and pepper to taste.

When the coals are ready or the gas grill is hot, grill the lamb pieces for 8 to 9 minutes, turning so that each side is uniformly done. They should be medium-rare.

While the lamb is cooking, put the saucepan with the *picadillo* sauce in a corner of the grill and let the sauce heat up.

When the lamb is done, remove the meat from the skewers to a large, shallow bowl. Pour the warmed *picadillo* sauce over it and toss so that all the pieces are covered. Transfer to a platter and serve immediately, garnished with chopped scallions or parsley or both.

So Many Ingredients = So Much Time?

NEVER BE PUT OFF by the length of an ingredients list. Afterward, you may decide that the recipe was way too difficult and be happy that some honey dripped on that page of the cookbook, because now it is stuck to another page and you will never have to see that recipe again. But this kind of recipe meltdown usually occurs because of some labor-intensive prep work or some odd timing requiring you to commit several hours one day and more hours the next and then set your alarm on the third day. Rarely is it the number of ingredients that go into the dish that is so confounding.

As you start using this and other cookbooks, you will begin to see patterns in the recipes. The last six ingredients might be a similar set of spices. I include several that end by adding some combination of chili powder, paprika, ground cumin, dried oregano, brown sugar, salt, and pepper, a pattern that appears with some regularity in other grilling books as well. This means that the last inch of the ingredients list doesn't involve much labor.

The real problem with an ingredients list, regardless of length, occurs when you don't have something on hand that you need. You are now faced with a huge decision. Do you make do, or do you run out and get what's missing? It's fourth down and short—do you go for it or do you punt?

Of course, much depends on what you're missing and how far you have to go to get it. If you need cream and there's a grocery on the corner, go for it. If it's dried oregano and you have to drive to get it, punt. I can't stress enough, though, how important it is to spend the time to put an accurate shopping list together, knowing that every ingredient is important. Like anything, once you get in the habit, it will become second nature.

So do not blanch at what might at first seem like a long list of ingredients. It may turn out to be the easiest recipe to prepare.

Grilled Lamb Shanks

This is another braise/grill combo that brings out the best of both techniques. You get the deep flavor and soft, luscious texture from the braising and the smoky char and delectable crust from the fire. And like most braised dishes, the flavor actually improves with a day in the refrigerator. Make the lamb shanks on a Sunday afternoon—brown them during the pregame show (no one feels good about themselves when watching the pregame show anyway—it's as though you *really* have nothing better to do with your life), start the braising process just before kickoff, turn off the heat and let them cool after the third quarter, and then, at the end of the game, either put them in the fridge for another night or start thinking about firing up the grill. **Serves** 4

Ingredients

2 tablespoons extra virgin olive oil

4 lamb shanks, each about 1 pound

1 medium onion, finely chopped

1 carrot, peeled and finely chopped

1 cup port or red wine

8 cloves garlic (don't bother to peel them)

1 tablespoon fresh rosemary,
  or 1 teaspoon dried

1 tablespoon fresh thyme,
  or 1 teaspoon dried

Salt and freshly ground black pepper

→ **Place** an 8-quart Dutch oven over high heat, add the oil, and heat until it just starts smoking. Carefully brown the lamb shanks on all sides, taking your time to get a deep golden brown; this should take 10 to 15 minutes. Remove the meat and set aside. Lower the heat slightly, add the onions and carrots to the pan, and cook until lightly browned and soft, about 8 minutes.

Add the wine, garlic, rosemary, and thyme and bring to a boil. Add the meat. Reduce the heat to low, cover, and simmer gently for 2 hours, or until the meat is soft and almost falling off the bone.

Remove the shanks and strain the sauce into a medium saucepan. If time allows, refrigerate both separately, so you can skim the fat from the top of the sauce.

Prepare enough coals for a hot charcoal fire, or preheat your gas grill on high for 10 minutes with the lid closed.

When the coals are ready or the gas grill is hot, grill the lamb shanks until they are nicely browned all over, sprinkling them with salt and pepper to taste and turning as necessary, about 12 minutes.

While the lamb is cooking, put the saucepan with the sauce in a corner of the grill and let it heat up.

Transfer the shanks to a platter and cover with the sauce. Serve immediately.

Father's Day Lamb Chops

I always start off with the best intentions that this will be the year I let my wife and kids cook me a nice Father's Day dinner. But then somehow I wind up at the butcher, chatting about this and that, and the next thing I know I'm picking out a phalanx of thick-cut lamb chops that I will wind up grilling myself. I know I should be more receptive to change, but Father's Day wouldn't be the same without lamb chops and, well, I *do* cook them exactly the way I like them, and it *is* Father's Day after all, my one (and only) day of the year, so why shouldn't I get to eat what I want. Huh? **Serves** 4

Ingredients

8 loin lamb chops, about 1 inch thick

2 tablespoons extra virgin olive oil

¼ cup chopped garlic

1 tablespoon chopped fresh rosemary

2 teaspoons chopped fresh thyme

Salt and freshly ground black pepper

➔ **Arrange** the lamb chops on a platter and brush both sides with olive oil. Mix together the garlic, rosemary, thyme, and salt and pepper to taste; spread the mixture evenly over both sides of each of the chops. The chops can sit at room temperature while the coals are getting hot.

Prepare enough coals for a hot charcoal fire, or preheat your gas grill on high for 10 minutes with the lid closed.

When the coals are ready or the gas grill is hot, grill the lamb chops for 9 to 11 minutes, turning once, until they are medium-rare.

Transfer to a platter and let them rest for 5 minutes before serving.

What I Want for Father's Day

YOU KNOW, it would really be okay this year to skip the socks. I still have in my drawer, unworn, the ones from last year, with the magenta stripes that probably looked really cool in the store but on my ankles resemble a baboon's behind. In fact, I have the socks from the year before that as well. And I'll take a pass on another tie, since those I've received in the past appear to have been chosen for me under deep duress—how else to explain the leitmotif of swans or the brace of mallards in midflight? Likewise, ix-nay on any wrenches or wallets. After a quick inventory, I feel I'm good to go in both departments. I could open my own store. And no go on the shaver, the electric back massager, the monogrammed leather dopp kit. Really. It's okay. I'll manage somehow.

But there is something I actually want this year, though it can't be bought or wrapped. What I truly want for Father's Day, this one special day of the year designated for me—Dad—is for The Progeny to laugh at my jokes. And by that I mean a *real* laugh, not the derisive one I usually get or any of the ersatz laughs that spring from pity, as though I'm fraught with midlife crises and not laughing might bring on a crying jag. No. On this one day I want genuine laughs. As if something truly funny was being said—something archly insightful and witty and unbearably funny. I want laughs whether there's a punch line or not. Off the cuff is not required. My zingers don't need to zing.

Q. What do you call a boomerang that doesn't come back?

A. A stick.

They've heard it before, but they have to laugh like they haven't. I want big yuks. I want boffo. Because on this one day, *my* day, I want to feel like a young Bill Cosby, Steve Martin with an arrow through his head, Richard Pryor on the Sunset Strip knocking 'em dead. Laughs tumbling over each other. I'm working the room. I'm haloed in rim shots.

Stop it, Pop. You're killing us!

And my stories, too, are to be greeted with respect and reverence. I want knowing chuckles, subtle but deeply felt nods of the head, suggesting that my tales mean something, that they are *poignant*, they have *significance*—like the time in college when I spoke at the antiwar rally, or the mysterious old woman expatriate I met on the Spanish Steps in Rome, or the time I opened the camera to find the film missing and then a week later the photos arrived in the mail!

These stories should induce "ooohs" of wonder, "ahhhs" of awe. I want looks of deep and profound revelation, a sign that lets me know that someday in The Progeny's future, the lessons of their father's experiences will serve as guidance, something like wisdom as they confront the important decisions of their lives. A tear or two wouldn't be bad. Is that asking for too much?

It's no one's fault but my own that I am in this conundrum. There's even an acronym for it in my house—NFD. It stands for "Not Funny, Dad." It is uttered with disdainful regularity by The Progeny in response to my clever observations that, apparently, are not nearly as clever as I perceived them to be. My edgy witticisms have lost their edge. My *bon mots* are not so *bon*. The result—NFD.

I know I'm not alone here. I suffer from a curious malady peculiar to dads—the inexplicable compulsion to try to be funny. Moms are generally immune to this quirky and aberrant behavior. They don't seem to need to crack jokes with waiters in restaurants—they are weirdly content just to order. Moms don't sit at the table when their kids have friends for dinner and try to sound hip by brazenly employing lingo without knowing whether the words are nouns or adjectives. Moms just ask benign questions like, "What are your summer plans?"

I'll cook my own Father's Day dinner. I'll even do the dishes. No problem there. But if we're out, say, having lunch at a Thai restaurant and I spill some curry sauce on my shirt, when I remark, "Hey, I'm wearing my Father's Day Thai," I'm expecting spit takes. I want green tea sprayed across the table.

And then there will be no rolling of the eyes, no hiding faces behind a hand to disguise pained looks of weariness. No "Honey, give it a rest." No "Nice try, Dad." Cringing is forbidden this Father's

Day. As is spiriting friends away, like I'm an object of shame, like I'm wearing a scarlet "A." The only "A" is for my "A" material, which I have—all day, *my* day.

Ba-dum-bum-ching.

Because this is Father's Day and Dad gets cut a little joke slack. I'm on. I'm not dyin' out there. I'm on a roll.

I'm *not* dyin' out there.

Two sausages in a frying pan. One says to the other, "Man, it's hot in here." The other sausage says, "Whattaya know, a talking sausage!!"

"Thank you. Thank you very much. I'll be here 'til the end of the day."

Lamb & Merguez Kabobs with Mint Yogurt Sauce

I once asked a bunch of chefs I know to name one ingredient that, when they used it, it felt like cheating. One said "really incredible olive oil," which, when poured liberally over, say, a grilled chicken breast turns it into something wonderful. Another extolled sea salt. Another chose fennel pollen, as expensive as saffron and, when sprinkled on plain pasta and butter, transforms it into an exotic experience. My vote goes to *merguez*, the spicy Moroccan lamb sausage that is pungently seasoned with garlic, cayenne, cumin, black pepper, paprika, cinnamon, cloves, and allspice. Because the sausage itself contains so much flavor, when you cook with it you don't need to do much else. Find some at a local gourmet shop and you'll be able to start cheating, too. **Serves** 4

Ingredients

8 **bamboo skewers**

1 **teaspoon curry powder**

1 **teaspoon ground cinnamon**

½ **teaspoon ground nutmeg**

1 **teaspoon salt**

1½ **pounds boneless lamb from the shoulder, cut into 1-inch cubes**

2 **tablespoons extra virgin olive oil**

8 **ounces merguez sausage, cut into ¾-inch pieces**

1 **medium red onion, peeled and cut into 1-inch pieces**

Mint Yogurt Sauce (recipe on facing page)

→ **One** hour before grilling, soak the bamboo skewers in warm water.

In a small bowl, combine the curry powder, cinnamon, nutmeg, and salt. Place the lamb cubes in a large bowl and pour the olive oil over them. Add the spices and mix so that all the cubes are evenly coated.

Prepare enough coals for a hot charcoal fire, or preheat your gas grill on high for 10 minutes with the lid closed.

While the coals are heating up, thread the lamb cubes, merguez, and onion pieces onto the skewers, about 2 each per skewer, making sure not to crowd them too closely.

When the coals are ready or the gas grill is hot, grill the kabobs for 8 to 9 minutes, turning them several times so they cook evenly, until they are medium-rare.

Transfer the skewers to a serving platter and serve with the Mint Yogurt Sauce.

Mint Yogurt Sauce

Easy to make, this combo of mint and yogurt provides a refreshing accompaniment to the kabobs.

Makes about 1 cup

Ingredients

1 cup whole milk yogurt

½ medium cucumber, peeled, seeded, and coarsely grated

3 tablespoons chopped fresh mint

1 tablespoon fresh lemon juice

1 clove garlic, finely chopped

½ teaspoon ground coriander

½ teaspoon ground cumin

Salt and freshly ground black pepper

→ **Stir** together the yogurt, cucumber, mint, lemon juice, garlic, coriander, and cumin in a medium bowl. Season with salt and pepper to taste. Cover and refrigerate until ready to use. The sauce will keep in the refrigerator for up to 3 days.

How to Properly De-Skewer

THERE ARE TWO WAYS to get food off a skewer—one works well, the other less so.

NO: Do not position your fork behind the bottom piece of meat on the skewer and try to push the meat away from you. This is surprisingly difficult and could result in the kabob components flying in places that you didn't intend.

YES: Instead, position your fork behind the bottom piece of meat and pull the skewer toward you. Because of some law of physics I don't understand, this technique permits the skewer to move freely, and the meat and vegetables drop demurely onto the waiting platter.

Don't Push

Pull!

Grilled Chipotle Leg of Lamb

The grill does something wonderful with these traditional Mexican flavors, searing them into the lamb to give it a deep, smoky flavor. It's not how you would usually expect leg of lamb to be done, but you will receive accolades from all who try it.

Serves 6 to 8

Ingredients

1 medium onion, coarsely chopped

7 cloves garlic, coarsely chopped

1 cup jarred green tomatillo salsa

¼ cup chicken broth

2 chipotle chiles in adobo, seeded and chopped (see Note)

1 teaspoon chili powder

1 teaspoon sugar

1 teaspoon kosher salt, plus more for grilling

½ teaspoon ground cinnamon

Pinch grated nutmeg

1 leg of lamb (6 to 7 pounds), boned, butterflied, and the fat trimmed

Freshly ground black pepper

→ **Place** the onion, garlic, salsa, chicken broth, chipotles, chili powder, sugar, 1 teaspoon salt, cinnamon, and nutmeg in the container of a food processor or blender and pulse until the mixture is smooth. Rub half the paste onto both sides of the lamb, reserving the remaining marinade. Let the lamb rest at room temperature for 30 minutes, or cover it and refrigerate for least 2 hours or up to 12 hours. Bring the lamb to room temperature before grilling.

Prepare enough coals for a medium-hot charcoal fire, or preheat your gas grill on medium-high for 10 minutes with the lid closed.

When the coals are ready or the gas grill is hot, season the lamb with salt and pepper to taste and grill for about 12 minutes, until the bottom is nicely browned. Turn and grill for 12 minutes more. Brush the lamb with the reserved marinade, turning it a few more times in the last few minutes. The meat thermometer should register 145°F at the thickest part for medium-rare.

Transfer the lamb to a platter and let it rest for 10 minutes under an aluminum foil tent, then slice and serve.

Note: *Chipotle chiles come in a can with adobo sauce. They are pretty hot, so you probably want to get rid of the seeds, which is where most of the heat resides. Wash your hands well with soap after working with the chipotles. You can use chipotle chiles in moderation in any dish with a Mexican flavor to add heat and complexity.*

The center portion of the butterflied leg is thinner than the two end sections (it resembles a slightly squashed dumbbell). When the thinner center section is medium-rare, use a sharp knife to trim it off, letting the two thicker, more bulbous end sections cook for about 5 minutes longer.

Sea Salt? *Si!*

HOW, YOU ASK, when there are so many expenses in your life; when the price of just waking up in the morning seems to rise every day; when college tuition is looming, as are braces, ski equipment, and designer jeans whose sole claim to being "designed" is 12 cents' worth of gold thread sewn in a seemingly random, slightly deranged pattern on the back pockets; when lessons for things you remember doing on your own—for *fun*—now apparently require the advice and counsel of a (very expensive) "expert"; and when you're faced every month by a crippling bill for the family cell phones, whose singular purpose seems to be to provide an opportunity for The Progeny to lie in bed indulging in inane gossip, which they could easily do for a tenth of the price on a Princess phone plugged into the wall; *how*, you wonder, can I seriously suggest you pay almost $10 for a handful of salt? *Salt*, which they give away at every restaurant and lunch counter. You are probably filled with the same righteous disdain Allen Iverson showed for practice.

Practice?
Salt???

But—and you knew that was coming, that *but*—you can do yourself no better culinary favor than to shell out that sawbuck for some real sea salt, harvested by hand, its granules, relative to the free-flowing salt you're used to, gigantic and bursting with a flavor that both supports and enhances whatever it is being used on. The difference is like the moment when *The Wizard of Oz* goes from black and white to color.

I actually keep a constant supply of two sea salts, and not because I am being courted by the salt lobby. One is a dusky-hued French one, and the other, also from France, is a mixture of sea salt and *herbes de Provence*. I can simply roast some potatoes or scramble some unadulterated eggs or throw a naked steak on the grill, but when I finish it off with one of these two salts, and maybe drizzle on a little olive oil, I assure you that anyone I place it in front of is dazzled. So get some real and expensive sea salt in your life, and you will elevate your cooking in a startling way, with absolutely no extra effort.

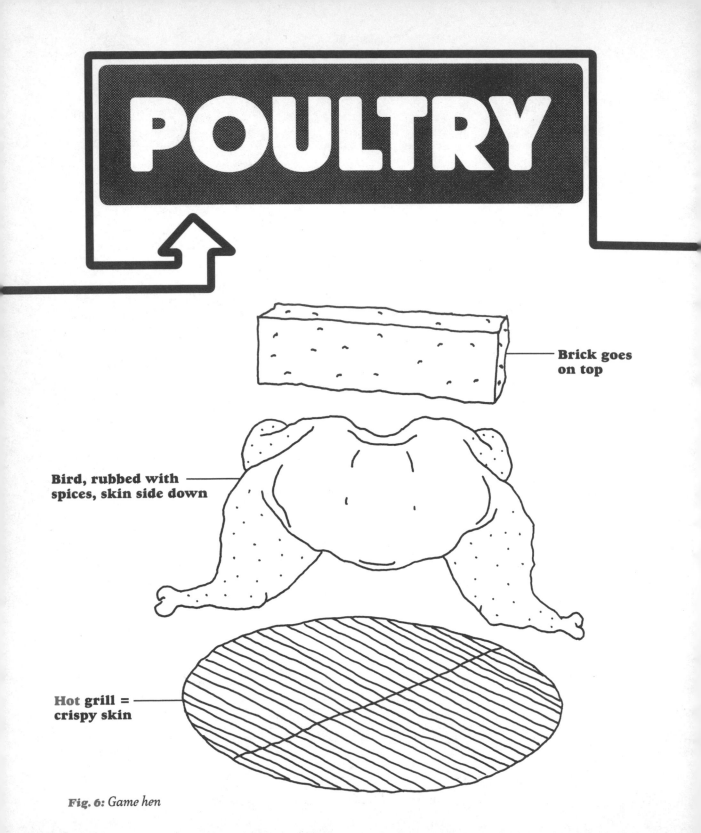

POULTRY

Brick goes on top

Bird, rubbed with spices, skin side down

Hot grill = crispy skin

Fig. 6: Game hen

06

Back in the older, simpler days, before the designated hitter and the West Coast Offense, people used to cook a chicken by taking a chicken, putting it in the oven, and cooking it.

Once roasted, it would be cut with a big pair of kitchen shears into different pieces and served with some gravy enhanced with a few teaspoons of Kitchen Magic. But the challenge that always comes with cooking a whole chicken is how to get the dark meat (which takes longer) to cook through without overcooking the white meat. (That's where the gravy came into play, smothering the dried-out white meat with a sauce so thick and unctuous you couldn't tell where it ended and the chicken began.)

Then the chicken industry started to see the whole chicken as something that could be Balkanized and sold in pieces. In your supermarket's poultry section you can now find several choices of packaged chicken units, many of which are impossible to distinguish as having once belonged to a chicken or, for that matter, any living thing.

Like most modern conveniences, this makes Dad's job both simpler and more complicated at the same time. Now, instead of just chicken, Dad has to decipher the arsenal of chicken packages—thighs with skin, without skin, bone-in or boneless; whole boneless breasts, sliced boneless breasts, boneless breast tenderloins. But the choices do allow Dad to barbecue with a little more equanimity, knowing that his grill is not the venue for partisan wrangling. If the breasts need to be removed before the thighs, then that can be easily accommodated.

One reason breasts need less time is that they are leaner than thighs and, hence, cook through more quickly. It also means that whatever flavor there is in the breast can easily be lost through overcooking. Chicken breasts, like pork chops, must be removed from the grill as soon as they are cooked through. This will help keep them moist and flavorful. Even a few extra minutes' cooking time will make you wonder why you bothered making them in the first place.

Dad's Awesome Grilling Book

Barbecued Game Hens "Under the Brick"

This is the traditional way of cooking small chickens in Tuscany, though of course the bricks they use are metric. Having the weight on the hens while they grill makes the skin extra crispy and really amps up the flavor. Have one of The Progeny on hand in the vicinity of the grill to perform the ceremonial laying on of the bricks. **Serves** 4

Ingredients

1 bunch fresh basil

¼ cup dried rosemary

2 tablespoons paprika

¼ cup freshly ground black pepper

¼ cup salt

¼ to ½ cup extra virgin olive oil

4 Rock Cornish game hens or baby chickens (called *poussins*), backbones removed (have your butcher do this, if possible)

4 standard bricks wrapped in foil

2 lemons, cut into wedges, for garnish

→ **Place** the basil, rosemary, paprika, black pepper, salt, and ¼ cup of the olive oil in the container of a food processor or blender and pulse several times, until it becomes a smooth paste. Add more oil, a tablespoon at a time, if necessary. Rub both sides of the birds with the basil mixture and let them sit in the refrigerator for least 2 hours or up to 12 hours.

When you are ready to cook the birds, prepare enough coals for a two-tiered fire, hot on one side, medium on the other, or preheat your gas grill on medium-high on one side and medium on the other for 10 minutes with the lid closed.

When the coals are ready or the gas grill is hot, arrange the hens, skin side down, on the hot side of the grill and place a foil-wrapped brick on top of each one. Do not move them for 8 minutes. If a flare-up occurs, cover the grill briefly until it goes out. Turn the hens over, place the bricks on top, and cook for 8 minutes more on the hot side of the grill.

Transfer the hens to the medium side of the grill and cook, skin side up, for 10 more minutes. Turn and cook for another 10 to 12 minutes, until the hens are just cooked through and a thermometer inserted into the thickest part of the thigh reads 170°F.

Transfer the hens to a platter and serve immediately with the lemon wedges.

Mexican Wedding Chicken Mole

To give you an idea of how tasty this is, it's the first recipe that the oldest of The Progeny wanted to learn. Good mole takes your breath away with its refined balance of sweet and spice. On a family trip to the Yucatán, the local mole was deemed only slightly better than Dad's, which I took as no small accomplishment. **Serves** 4

Ingredients

3 **dried ancho chiles (see Note)**

1 **dried New Mexico chile**

2 **tablespoons vegetable oil**

1 **medium onion, finely chopped**

2 **cloves garlic, finely chopped**

¼ **cup raisins**

3 **tablespoons slivered almonds**

3 **tablespoons pumpkin seeds**

2 **tablespoons sesame seeds, plus more for garnish**

1 **tablespoon chili powder**

½ **teaspoon ground coriander**

½ **teaspoon ground cumin**

1 **tablespoon honey**

1 **teaspoon unsweetened cocoa powder**

Salt and freshly ground black pepper

½ **cup tomato purée**

1 **cup water**

2½ **pounds boneless chicken thighs**

12 **corn tortillas, for serving**

→ **Remove** the stems and seeds from the chiles, tear them into roughly 2-inch pieces, and soak the pieces in 2 cups very hot water for 30 minutes. Reserve the soaking liquid.

Place a large, heavy-bottomed skillet over medium-high heat. When the pan gets hot, add the oil, spreading it so it evenly coats the bottom of the pan. Add the onions and cook, stirring regularly, until they soften, about 7 minutes. Add the garlic and cook for 1 minute more.

Add the raisins, almonds, pumpkin seeds, sesame seeds, chili powder, coriander, cumin, honey, cocoa powder, and salt and pepper to taste, and stir so the spices toast a bit, about 1 minute.

Lift the reconstituted chiles from the liquid and add them to the skillet, along with the tomato purée, ½ cup of the liquid the chiles were soaked in, and the 1 cup water.

Bring the sauce to a boil, reduce the heat to low, and cook on a low simmer, partially covered, for 16 minutes.

Let the mole cool, then transfer it in batches to the container of a food processor or blender and purée until it becomes a smooth, slightly thick sauce. Adjust the seasoning with salt and honey, a half teaspoon at a time, until the taste is to your liking.

Transfer the mole to a medium saucepan and set aside, or place in a plastic container and refrigerate for up to 2 days.

Prepare enough coals for a hot charcoal fire, or preheat your gas grill on high for 10 minutes with the lid closed. Season the chicken thighs on both sides with salt and pepper.

When the coals are ready or the gas grill is hot, grill the chicken thighs for 9 to 10 minutes, turning once, until they are cooked through.

While the chicken is cooking, place the saucepan in a corner of the grill to heat up the mole.

Transfer the cooked chicken to a platter. Top with the mole and garnish with a small handful of sesame seeds. Serve with corn tortillas.

Note: *To make this mole, you will need to bring dried chile peppers into your life. They are sold in small packages and come in many different varieties and levels of heat. They look a little foreboding, as they resemble the bark of an old tree rather than anything anyone would want to eat, but you will get used to them. Ancho and New Mexico chiles are two of the mildest varieties. Like all dried chiles, they require a 30-minute soak in a bath of very hot water to revive them and make them pliable. As with fresh chile peppers, the heat is contained primarily in the seeds and ribs. Cut the peppers open and remove the stems. Shake out all the seeds you can and trim away the ribs if they are easily accessible with a paring knife. The peppers are now ready to be reconstituted. More advanced mole recipes will have you toast the dried chile peppers in a heavy-bottomed skillet over high heat for about 40 seconds to accentuate their flavor. Feel free to do this if you like.*

The Wedding Trick

LIKE MANY RECIPES in my repertoire, this is one is not absolutely authentic. A mole maven would no doubt spot several unmole-like procedures I employ. But I'll let you in on a little secret—my clandestine strategy for compensating for any lack of authenticity. When I describe the dish, I make sure to use the word "wedding."

My mole recipe, for instance, isn't really "Mexican Wedding Mole," but when you invoke that word—wedding—it immediately conjures up a group of joyous folks celebrating together, relishing the food prepared by grandmothers whose estimable cooking skills are only that much more enhanced by the joy and love that inspires them on this wondrous day. No one's going to say anything bad about any dish that has the word "wedding" in it.

"Hey, this isn't *real* mole."

"Yes, I know. It's *wedding* mole."

End of discussion.

Try it out yourself: Jamaican Wedding Jerk Pork; Japanese Wedding Miso-Ginger Grilled Salmon; Thai Wedding Grilled Beef. Your guests will be instantly filled with a spirit of warmth and generosity.

So remember, dads, when in doubt, throw the word "wedding" into the recipe title and half your work is done.

Chicken Fingers with Spicy Peanut Sauce

It's not odd that kids love chicken fingers, but it *is* a little odd that kids love something *called* chicken fingers. Because if you take a moment to think about the chicken/fingers concept, it's somewhat disconcerting. Say it slowly: "I'm eating chicken fingers." You see what I mean? Nevertheless, this version is a favorite of The Progeny because of the hint of coconut on the chicken and the spicy peanut dipping sauce, which is slightly addictive. Broccoli even takes on a whole new and dynamic presence when dipped in it. **Serves 4**

Ingredients

Half a small onion, sliced

2 cloves garlic, coarsely chopped

1 tablespoon coarsely chopped fresh ginger

1 tablespoon red curry paste

1 cup coconut milk

2 tablespoons rice vinegar

1 tablespoon soy sauce

2 tablespoons sugar

½ teaspoon salt

1 pound skinless, boneless chicken breast, cut into strips about 1½ inches wide

Spicy Peanut Sauce (recipe on facing page), for dipping

→ **Place** the onion, garlic, ginger, red curry paste, coconut milk, rice vinegar, soy sauce, sugar, and salt in the container of a food processor or blender and pulse until the mixture is smooth.

Place the chicken strips in a bowl or plastic container just large enough to hold them and add the coconut milk mixture. Let the chicken marinate in the refrigerator for at least 1 hour and up to 8 hours.

Prepare enough coals for a hot charcoal fire, or preheat your gas grill on high for 10 minutes with the lid closed.

When the coals are ready or the gas grill is hot, grill the chicken strips for 3 minutes, until they're just golden brown. Turn and grill for about 3 minutes more, until they are just cooked through.

Transfer to a platter and serve with a bowl of the Spicy Peanut Sauce.

Spicy Peanut Sauce

A little heat, a touch of sweetness,
and the tangy peanut flavor make
this dip irresistible.

Makes about ¾ cup

Ingredients

½ **cup natural chunky peanut butter,
at room temperature**

¼ **cup warm water, plus more as needed**

2 **tablespoons brown sugar**

1 **tablespoon soy sauce**

1 **teaspoon sesame oil**

¼ **teaspoon cayenne pepper**

→ **Stir** all the ingredients together in a small
bowl until well combined. Add more warm
water, ½ teaspoon at a time, to achieve a diplike
consistency. Set aside or transfer to a plastic
container and refrigerate for up to 4 days.
Let the sauce come to room temperature before
serving.

Grilled Quail

The Progeny get a kick out of these little birds. Each gets a pair and they get to play Fred Flintstone, eating with their fingers, relishing the tasty meat that slips off the bone. It's better if you can marinate these overnight. **Serves** 4

Ingredients

½ **cup extra virgin olive oil**

¼ **cup balsamic vinegar**

4 **cloves garlic, thinly sliced**

1 **teaspoon fennel seeds**

1 **tablespoon chopped fresh thyme, or 1 teaspoon dried**

1 **teaspoon chopped fresh or dried rosemary**

2 **teaspoons salt**

1 **teaspoon freshly ground black pepper**

8 **quail, sleeve-boned (rib bones removed; ask the butcher to do this)**

4 **lemons, cut in half widthwise**

→ **In** a medium bowl, mix together the oil, vinegar, garlic, fennel seeds, thyme, rosemary, salt, and pepper until just combined.

Place the quail in a large, resealable freezer bag and add the marinade. Let the quail marinate for at least 4 hours and up to 24 hours.

Prepare enough coals for a hot charcoal fire, or preheat your gas grill on high for 10 minutes with the lid closed.

When the coals are ready or the gas grill is hot, grill the quail for 4 minutes, until are they just golden brown. Turn and grill for 3 to 4 minutes more, until they are cooked through. While the quail are finishing, place the lemon halves, cut sides down, on the outer edge of the grill for 2 minutes.

Transfer the quail and lemons to a platter and serve immediately.

Chicken Thighs Cubano

Cuban cooking features a rhythm section of citrus on piano, garlic on percussion, and some gentle but persistent heat on bass. Which reminds me: Preparation of this dish would be the perfect time to introduce The Progeny to some classic Cuban music. Start with the *Buena Vista Social Club* album and see where that leads you. **Serves** 4

Ingredients

12 chicken thighs (about 3 pounds)

½ cup fresh lime juice

¼ cup grapefruit juice

¼ cup extra virgin olive oil

½ cup chopped fresh cilantro

4 cloves garlic, finely chopped

1 tablespoon chopped fresh thyme

2 teaspoons seeded, chopped jalapeño chile

2 teaspoons Hungarian sweet paprika

2 teaspoons freshly ground black pepper

1 teaspoon ground cumin

½ teaspoon salt

→ **Place** the chicken thighs in a plastic container just large enough to hold them.

In a medium bowl, mix together the lime juice, grapefruit juice, olive oil, cilantro, garlic, thyme, jalapeño, paprika, black pepper, cumin, and salt. Pour two-thirds of the marinade over the chicken thighs, and maneuver them so they are all evenly coated. Cover and refrigerate for at least 1 hour and up to 4 hours. Set aside the remaining marinade.

Prepare enough coals for a hot charcoal fire, or preheat your gas grill on high for 10 minutes with the lid closed.

When the coals are ready or the gas grill is hot, grill the chicken thighs for 4 minutes, until just golden brown. Turn and grill for 3 to 4 minutes more, until they are cooked through. Mop the thighs on both sides with the reserved marinade during the last 2 minutes of cooking.

Transfer the chicken thighs to a platter and serve immediately.

Chicken Sandwiches

These are the best chicken sandwiches ever. You can make these the centerpiece of a spectacular lunch, perhaps in celebration of the day when it's finally warm enough to set up the hammock. These sammies are also substantial enough to serve for dinner, as The Progeny have been known to bug me to do. Some chips and slaw and a grilled ear of corn make for a casual and fun change-of-pace evening meal for summer.

Makes 4 sandwiches

Ingredients

4 skinless, boneless chicken breast halves

3 medium zucchini, trimmed and cut lengthwise into ⅓-inch-thick slices

1 large red onion, cut into ⅓-inch-thick slices

¼ cup extra virgin olive oil

Salt and freshly ground black pepper

4 ounces Cheddar cheese, sliced

4 kaiser rolls

¼ cup mayonnaise

4 ounces prosciutto, thinly sliced

8 tomato slices

→ **Place** the chicken breasts, zucchini, and onion slices on a large platter. Brush both sides with olive oil and season to taste with salt and pepper.

Prepare enough coals for a medium-hot charcoal fire, or preheat your gas grill on medium-high for 10 minutes with the lid closed.

When the coals are ready or the gas grill is hot, grill the chicken, zucchini, and onion for 5 minutes. Turn, laying slices of Cheddar on the chicken breasts, and cook for 4 to 5 minutes more, until the chicken is just cooked through and the zucchini is a deep brown. The zucchini may cook a little faster, so be attentive to it.

Transfer everything to a platter. Split the rolls, and spread the mayonnaise on them. Place a chicken breast on the bottom half of each roll. Top with a slice of prosciutto, some slices of grilled zucchini and onion and fresh tomato, followed by the top half of the roll. Serve immediately.

Sesame Chicken Drumsticks

These are just plain fun. The Progeny are always keen for me to grill up a mess o' drumsticks when they have friends coming for dinner. Besides tasting great, they are perfect served at room temperature. That means you don't have to worry if the Wiffle ball game goes into extra innings. Just lay a clean kitchen towel over the platter of grilled drumsticks and let them sit until the last out. Also keep these in mind if you're headed to a picnic or have to bring something to a lakeside potluck. **Serves** 4

Ingredients

3 pounds chicken drumsticks

⅓ cup soy sauce

¼ cup mirin rice wine, or white wine plus 1 teaspoon honey

2 tablespoons sesame oil

1 tablespoon vegetable oil

2 tablespoons brown sugar

4 cloves garlic, finely chopped

2 tablespoons finely chopped fresh ginger, or 1 teaspoon ground ginger

¼ cup sesame seeds, for garnish

→ **Place** the chicken drumsticks in a plastic container just large enough to hold them. In a medium bowl, mix together the soy sauce, wine, sesame oil, vegetable oil, brown sugar, garlic, and ginger. Pour two-thirds of the marinade over the drumsticks, and maneuver them so they are all evenly coated. Cover and refrigerate for at least 1 hour and up to 4 hours. Set aside the remaining marinade.

Prepare enough coals for a hot charcoal fire, or preheat your gas grill on high for 10 minutes with the lid closed.

When the coals are ready or the gas grill is hot, grill the drumsticks for about 22 minutes, turning several times so they are browned evenly and cooked through. Mop the drumsticks with the reserved marinade during the last 4 minutes of cooking.

Transfer to a platter, sprinkle with the sesame seeds, and serve.

Greek Salad with Grilled Chicken

This dish makes for a swell summer lunch while lounging by the pool. If you don't have a pool, make an offer to a friend that you'll bring lunch if you can lounge by his.
Serves 4

Ingredients

½ **cup extra virgin olive oil**

2 **tablespoons red wine vinegar**

2 **tablespoons fresh lemon juice**

2 **tablespoons chopped fresh basil**

1 **tablespoon chopped fresh oregano, or 1 teaspoon dried**

2 **teaspoons finely chopped garlic**

½ **teaspoon salt**

Freshly ground black pepper

2 **tablespoons freshly grated Parmesan cheese**

1 **teaspoon sugar**

4 **skinless, boneless chicken breast halves, pounded thin**

8 **cups torn romaine lettuce**

1 **cucumber, peeled and sliced**

16 **pitted kalamata olives**

12 **ounces cherry tomatoes**

1 **red bell pepper, stemmed, seeded, and cut into roughly 1-inch pieces**

1 **small red onion, thinly sliced**

½ **cup crumbled feta cheese**

→ **In** a medium bowl, combine the olive oil, vinegar, lemon juice, basil, oregano, garlic, salt, pepper to taste, Parmesan, and sugar.

Place the chicken breasts on a platter and pour half of the dressing over them. Brush the chicken so each breast is coated evenly on both sides with the dressing.

Prepare enough coals for a hot charcoal fire, or preheat your gas grill on high for 10 minutes with the lid closed.

When the coals are ready or the gas grill is hot, grill the chicken breasts for 4 minutes, until they are golden brown. Turn and grill for 3 to 4 minutes more, until they are just cooked through.

Let the chicken breasts cool and cut them into
¼-inch slices. Transfer to a medium bowl
and let them sit at room temperature while you
finish the salad.

Combine the romaine, cucumber slices, olives,
cherry tomatoes, bell pepper, and red onion
in a salad bowl. Add ¼ cup of the remaining
dressing and toss together. Taste and add more
dressing if necessary. Top with the feta cheese
and chicken strips and serve.

Note: *You'll notice I had you pour the dressing onto
the chicken breasts rather than brush the dressing
on directly from the bowl. The reason for this is that
applying the brush to the raw chicken and then
dipping it back into the bowl might contaminate the
dressing. Always be aware of what implements or
surfaces come into contact with raw chicken, so they
are not used again before being washed in soapy
hot water.*

Grilled Chicken Parm

This is one of those recipes that makes people feel good, so save it for an occasion when someone in the household needs a little lift. Maybe one of The Progeny comes home from school feeling a little blue. Perhaps they does less than good than they wanted on a grammar test, or something like that; maybe. By the way, the cheese should flow, lavalike, off the edges of the chicken and will wind up messing up the grill, but that's why you have your grill brush. **Serves 4**

Ingredients

4 skinless, boneless chicken breast halves, pounded thin

2 tablespoons extra virgin olive oil

Salt and freshly ground black pepper

½ cup jarred pizza sauce

8 ounces mozzarella cheese, grated

¼ cup grated Parmesan cheese

→ **Brush** the chicken breasts on both sides with olive oil and season to taste with salt and pepper.

Prepare enough coals for a medium-hot charcoal fire, or preheat your gas grill on medium-high for 10 minutes with the lid closed.

When the coals are ready or the gas grill is hot, grill the chicken breasts for 4 minutes, until they are golden brown. Turn and immediately brush with the pizza sauce. Spread the mozzarella evenly on top of the sauce. Grill for 3 to 4 minutes more, until the breasts are just cooked through and the cheese has melted.

Transfer to a platter, sprinkle with the grated Parmesan, and serve immediately.

Note: *If, in addition to the grammar test, there was a less than stellar performance on a math quiz, you can lay a few slices of pepperoni over the pizza sauce before adding the mozzarella.*

Comino-Honey-Glazed Boneless Turkey Breast

I can't say enough about the striking flavor of this cumin-infused honey sauce and the ease with which it transforms a basic turkey breast into a truly spectacular dish. (It could easily become your new Thanksgiving main course.) And once you see how easy it is to basically turn honey into something so luxurious, you'll use it all the time.
Serves 6

Ingredients

1 cup honey, plus more for brushing

1 teaspoon ground cumin

½ teaspoon ground cinnamon

½ turkey breast, bone in (about 4 pounds)

Olive oil, for brushing turkey

Salt and coarsely ground black pepper

3 thick slices slab bacon

2 scallions, green parts only, finely chopped

1 chipotle chile in adobo, seeded and finely chopped

¼ cup chicken broth

→ **Combine** the 1 cup honey, cumin, and cinnamon in a small saucepan and warm over low heat. Remove from the heat and let sit at room temperature, covered, until ready to use, up to 2 days.

Prepare enough coals for a two-tiered fire, hot on one side, medium on the other, or preheat your gas grill on high on one side and medium on the other for 10 minutes with the lid closed. While the grill is heating, brush the turkey breast with olive oil and season well with salt and pepper.

When the coals are ready or the gas grill is hot, grill the turkey breast, skin side down, on the hot side of the grill until it is golden brown and a crust has formed, about 7 minutes. Turn the breast over, and transfer to the medium side of the grill. Close the cover and continue cooking until a meat thermometer inserted into the thickest part of the breast registers 165°F, 25 to

30 minutes. Brush the top with the honey several times during the last 10 minutes of cooking.

Remove the breast from the grill and let it rest, loosely tented with aluminum foil, for 10 minutes.

While the turkey breast is resting, lay the bacon slices across the grates of the grill for about 2 minutes per side, or until golden brown and slightly crunchy. Transfer to a plate lined with paper towels.

Place the saucepan with the comino honey on the grill. Break the bacon up into small pieces and add it to the saucepan, along with the scallions, chipotle chile, and chicken broth, and stir together. Heat until warmed through.

Cut the turkey breast into ¼-inch slices and arrange them on a platter. Cover with the warmed comino honey sauce and serve.

FISH & SEAFOOD

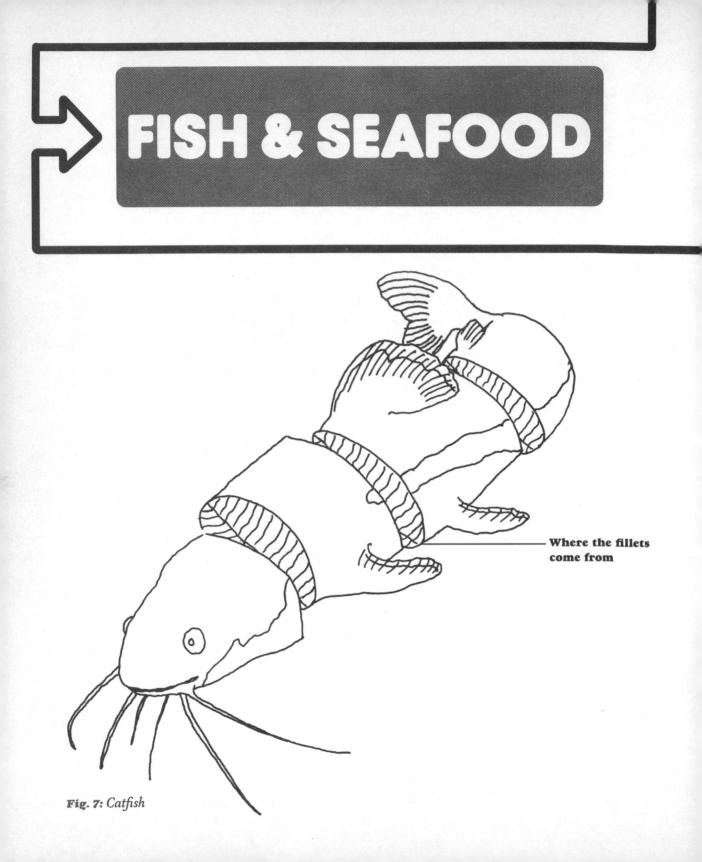

Where the fillets come from

Fig. 7: *Catfish*

Even if The Progeny believe in their heart of hearts that they don't like fish, they really can't make an informed judgment until they've had Dad's version.

It comes fresh off the grill, brazenly sporting a fabulous charred flavor and a killer crust that can be achieved only by cooking fish over an open flame.

Despite their reputation as being delicate and impossible to keep together on the grill, you can get fish fillets to do your bidding by following a few easy procedures:

1. Make sure the grill is clean.

2. Coat the fish liberally with spray cooking oil before grilling and then once again before turning it over. Get the nozzle in close to the fish on the grill so you don't initiate any flames.

3. Have an appropriately sized spatula, long and flexible enough to slip under the length of the fish and support it while you turn it over.

4. Let the grill grate get hot before placing the fish on it—this will help form a uniform crust that, besides enhancing the taste, will keep the fish from sticking.

5. Grill with the skin side down first. That way, when you pull the fish off the grill, the flesh will have just been on the grill and will be hot and wonderfully crispy.

6. Remember to keep raw and cooked seafood apart to prevent cross-contamination. After handling raw seafood, thoroughly wash your knives, your cutting surfaces, and your hands with hot, soapy water.

7. Always marinate fish or seafood in the refrigerator. Do not let the seafood or fish sit in an acidic marinade—with vinegar or lemon juice—for more than 30 minutes, as the acid will start to break it down.

8. Discard marinade after use. If you want to use the marinade to baste the seafood or fish on the grill, set some aside before marinating.

What to Look for When Buying Fish

The first thing to look for is a quality fish store. It will cost a little more, but you'll have a very good chance of getting really fresh fish. You can also ask questions and begin to develop some seafood savvy.

Here's what those in the know look for at the fish market:

Fresh whole fish should have:
1. A shiny surface with tightly adhering scales

2. Gills that are deep red or pink, free of slime, mucus, and off odors

3. A clean, shiny belly cavity, with no cuts or protruding bones

4. A mild aroma, similar to the ocean

5. Bright, clear eyes that seem full, not sunken or wrinkled

Fresh steaks, fillets, and loins should have:
1. A translucent look

2. Flesh that is firm and not separating

3. A mild odor, similar to the ocean

4. No discoloration

Grilled Halibut Reggio Emilia Style

Halibut is a great fish for the grill because it is so versatile and can take on so many different flavors. I first had this dish in the lovely Tuscan city of Reggio Emilia. It was served in that quaint little restaurant; you know the one—you get there by walking down that narrow, winding street and then up that even narrower alley, then going in an unmarked door practically hidden in the shadows, where they don't have a menu or even plates and it's been run for generations by the same family, whose ancestors arrived in Italy countless centuries ago after falling overboard off a Phoenician sailing vessel and then swimming to shore. The fish is served loaded with garlic and herbs that infuse it with flavor without being overpowering. **Serves 4**

Ingredients

½ **cup extra virgin olive oil**

2 cups packed fresh basil leaves

2 tablespoons fresh parsley leaves

3 cloves garlic, minced

2 tablespoons fresh lemon juice

2 teaspoons salt

2 teaspoons freshly ground black pepper

4 halibut steaks (6 ounces each)

Spray cooking oil

→ **Place** the olive oil, basil, parsley, garlic, lemon juice, salt, and pepper in the container of a food processor and pulse just until finely chopped. Transfer to a bowl and, if not using within a few hours, cover and refrigerate for up to 2 days.

Prepare enough coals for a hot charcoal fire, or preheat your gas grill on high for 10 minutes with the lid closed.

When the coals are ready or the gas grill is hot, spray one side of the halibut steaks liberally with cooking oil. Place on the grate, oiled side down, and grill for 5 to 6 minutes. Spray the tops of the steaks with oil, turn gently, and cook for 4 to 5 minutes more, until the center just becomes opaque.

Remove from the grill and transfer to dinner plates. Liberally spoon some of the basil-garlic pesto over the fish, and serve.

Salade Niçoise with Grilled Tuna

Ordinary salade niçoise is transformed by using fresh tuna. It's a cinch to cook, because you want to just char it on both sides and leave the center rare. That means you need to buy some high-quality, sushi-grade tuna at a really good fish market. How sexist is it for me to say that if your wife is hosting her book group or some other mysterious cabal of women that might assemble at your house you could prepare this salad for them? Well, I said it. **Serves** 4

Ingredients

1½ pounds tuna steaks, 1 inch thick

1¼ cups extra virgin olive oil

3 tablespoons red wine vinegar,
    or 2 tablespoons vinegar and
    1 tablespoon fresh lemon juice

2 tablespoons minced shallot

1 teaspoon Dijon-style mustard

1 large clove garlic, minced

1 anchovy, finely minced, or
    ½ teaspoon anchovy paste

2 tablespoons finely chopped fresh basil

1½ teaspoons minced fresh thyme,
    or ½ teaspoon dried

¼ teaspoon salt

Freshly ground black pepper

12 ounces green beans, trimmed

12 ounces fingerling or other
    small potatoes

12 ounces Boston lettuce (2 heads), leaves
    separated and torn into pieces

1 pint cherry or grape tomatoes

⅔ cup niçoise or other small, brine-cured
    black olives

→ **Place** the tuna steaks in a bowl just large enough to hold them, and add ½ cup of the olive oil. Make sure all sides of the tuna are coated with oil. Refrigerate until ready to grill, up to 4 hours.

In a small bowl, whisk together the vinegar, shallot, mustard, garlic, anchovy, basil, thyme, salt, and pepper to taste until well combined. Add the remaining ¾ cup oil in a slow stream, whisking as you do. Set the dressing aside, or cover and refrigerate for up to 4 days.

Cook the green beans in a medium saucepan in boiling salted water, uncovered, for 3 to 4 minutes, until they are al dente. Immediately transfer the beans with a slotted spoon to a large bowl of ice water to stop the cooking. Drain the beans, pat them dry, and set aside.

Simmer the potatoes in a medium saucepan for 15 to 20 minutes, until they are just cooked through. Drain in a colander and let cool. Cut in half while still slightly warm, and toss them in 2 tablespoons of the dressing in a medium bowl. Set aside.

Prepare enough coals for a hot charcoal fire, or preheat your gas grill on high for 10 minutes with the lid closed.

When the coals are ready or the gas grill is hot, grill the tuna for 3 minutes. Turn and grill for 3 to 4 minutes more, until the tuna is well browned but still rare inside.

Let the tuna stand for 3 minutes, then cut across the grain into ½–inch slices.

Arrange some lettuce leaves on 4 dinner plates. Lay some of the tuna slices across the center of the plate and arrange some tomatoes, green beans, potatoes, and olives around them. Drizzle dressing over the whole salad and serve with extra dressing on the side.

Grilled Cajun Catfish Fillets

Once The Progeny were old enough to embrace these seasonings, this was the first serious fish dish I served them. Needless to say, they liked it. Be aware, however, that Cajun Catfish is known as a "gateway fish." Once your progeny taste it, they may move on to more potent fish. It's just something you should be attentive to. **Serves** 4

Ingredients

¼ **cup peanut or other vegetable oil**

2 **tablespoons fresh lemon juice**

1½ **tablespoons Cajun or Creole seasoning**

½ **teaspoon salt**

4 **catfish fillets (1½ to 2 pounds total)**

Spray cooking oil

Lemon wedges, for serving

→ **Mix** together the oil, lemon juice, Cajun seasoning, and salt so they make a thick paste. Spread it on both sides of the fillets.

Prepare enough coals for a hot charcoal fire, or preheat your gas grill on high for 10 minutes with the lid closed.

When the coals are ready or the gas grill is hot, spray each fillet liberally with cooking oil and place, oiled side down, on the clean grill grate. Grill for 5 minutes. Spray the fillets again, turn gently, and grill for 4 to 5 minutes more, until they are just cooked through.

Serve with lemon wedges.

Trout Fillets in Foil

This is one of the easiest and best ways to cook fish for The Progeny. Grilling trout fillets in foil packets keeps in the flavor and produces a moist, perfectly cooked fish. And the strategic inclusion of a few pepperoni slices and some salsa is just added incentive to try it. **Serves** 4

Ingredients

Spray cooking oil

4 trout fillets

Salt

½ teaspoon freshly ground black pepper

1 cup favorite jarred salsa

12 slices pepperoni

→ **Cut** four 16-inch lengths of foil and lay them on a work surface. Spray with cooking oil.

Place a trout fillet in the center of each piece of foil and season with salt to taste and the pepper. Spoon 2 tablespoons of salsa over each trout fillet. Lay 3 pepperoni slices over the salsa on each fillet.

Bring the long ends of the foil together and fold them tightly several times. Then fold up the sides to make a neat, sealed packet.

Prepare enough coals for a hot charcoal fire, or preheat your gas grill on high for 10 minutes with the lid closed.

When the coals are ready or the gas grill is hot, lay the fish packets on the grill and cook for 14 minutes.

Open the packets carefully to avoid the escaping steam, and serve.

Grilled Pecan-Crusted Trout Fillets

The dusky sweetness of the molasses marinade and the nuttiness of the pecans make this unlike other fish dishes you've had. You'll need to be attentive to turning the fish to prevent the breading from scorching, but that's the only tricky part. This dish is featured at one of my favorite restaurants in the world—Hell's Backbone Grill in Boulder, Utah. Check it out when you take your family trip to Bryce Canyon.

Serves 4

Ingredients

⅓ **cup molasses**

⅓ **cup honey**

¼ **cup Dijon mustard**

3 **teaspoons chili powder**

4 **trout fillets**

1 **cup pecans, finely chopped**

1 **cup panko breadcrumbs**

1 **teaspoon salt**

½ **teaspoon cayenne pepper**

→ **Mix** together the molasses, honey, mustard, and 1 teaspoon of the chili powder. Brush the mixture liberally over the tops of the trout fillets and refrigerate for at least 1 hour and up to 4 hours.

Combine the pecans, breadcrumbs, remaining chili powder, salt, and cayenne in a wide shallow bowl. Lay the non-skin side of the fillets in the mixture so they are well coated. Then arrange them skin side down on a platter.

Prepare enough coals for a medium-hot charcoal fire, or preheat your gas grill on medium-high for 10 minutes with the lid closed.

When the coals are ready or the gas grill is hot, spray the non-skin-side of the fillet with cooking oil and place, oiled side down, on the clean grill grate. Cover the grill and cook for 2 to 3 minutes until the pecans turn dark brown. Spray the skin-side of the fillets, turn gently, and grill for 5 to 6 minutes more, until they are just cooked through.

Serve with lemon wedges.

Grilled Swordfish Kabobs with Pesto

Swordfish is one of my favorite fish to grill. And cooking it à la kabob helps to solve its major problem—keeping the lean swordfish meat from drying out. But even if you let it get a tad overcooked, the pesto makes up for it. Boil a few extra potatoes, which you can arrange on the grill next to the kabobs—they will be great with dinner or you can serve them cold the next day, topped with the pesto. **Serves** 4

Ingredients

8 **bamboo skewers**

2 **cups fresh basil leaves**

½ **cup fresh mint leaves**

½ **cup pine nuts**

1 **clove garlic, mashed**

½ **cup freshly grated Parmesan cheese**

2 **anchovy fillets**

1 **cup extra virgin olive oil**

2 **teaspoons fresh lemon juice**

1 **teaspoon salt**

¾ **teaspoon freshly ground black pepper**

1½ **pounds swordfish steaks, 1 inch thick, cut into 1½-inch cubes**

1 **red bell pepper, stemmed, seeded, and cut into 1-inch pieces**

1 **yellow bell pepper, stemmed, seeded, and cut into 1-inch pieces**

8 **small new potatoes, boiled until just tender (about 12 minutes)**

2 **small zucchini, about 1 inch thick, cut into ½-inch rounds**

Spray cooking oil

→ **One** hour before grilling, soak the bamboo skewers in warm water.

Place the basil and mint in the container of a food processor and pulse until finely chopped. Add the pine nuts, garlic, Parmesan, and anchovies and pulse a few more times until they are also chopped. With the machine running, add the oil in a thin, steady stream. Add the lemon juice, salt, and black pepper, and pulse to combine well. Transfer the pesto to a nonreactive bowl and set aside, covered

with plastic wrap, until ready to use, or refrigerate for up to 2 days, pressing a piece of plastic wrap directly over the top of the pesto.

Prepare enough coals for a hot charcoal fire, or preheat your gas grill on high for 10 minutes with the lid closed.

While the coals are heating up, thread the swordfish, red and yellow pepper pieces, potatoes, and zucchini onto the skewers, making sure not to crowd them.

Spray all sides of each kabob with oil.

When the coals are ready or the gas grill is hot, grill the swordfish kabobs for 8 to 9 minutes, turning them every 2 minutes or so to cook all the sides uniformly.

Transfer the kabobs to a platter and drizzle a liberal amount of the pesto over them; serve immediately.

Note: *This pesto makes up for any number of slip-ups. As long as you're not working in an Asian mode, throw a little pesto on something and it suddenly takes on a whole new glamour, like what happens when you put on your Armani suit. Make a double batch of pesto and store it in the freezer, portioned out in an ice cube tray. That way you can use just the amount you want.*

On Chopping

AT SOME POINT as you've been consulting this book, you've thought to yourself, "Hey, I thought this was a *grilling* book. I thought all I had to do was get the charcoal lit, unwrap something that looked very much like a steak, salt it, and cook it. How come there's so much chopping? What's that about?" You may feel a sense of betrayal and, consequently, search only for those recipes for which no chopping is required.

It's no solace, of course, for me to say that I understand. Let me just say this—a football game lasts around three hours, during which time about 18 minutes of actual football is played. Chopping is much the same. Purchasing all the ingredients, getting them home and put away, getting them out again when it's time to use them, making space on the counter, getting the cutting board set up—all that takes time. The chopping itself, when the knife is in direct contact with the foodstuff, actually goes quite quickly. It really does.

Getting a really good knife also helps. A premium, stainless steel blade that keeps its edge and sharpens easily will provide not only ease and safety but a measure of elegance and refinement to the chopping experience, like driving to the corner store for a quart of milk in your '68 Jaguar XKE.

I'm not going to encourage you to seek out the "Zen of chopping," nor am I going to challenge you to "be a man" and tough it out. But if you've ever gone surfing or skateboarding or downhill skiing, you know that the initial learning curve is steep, but once you find your balance, it becomes like second nature. The same will be true for chopping. The knife will become an extension of your hand and you will soon be chopping an onion with ease.

Grouper with Zesty Apricot Salsa

Grouper is a meaty, white–fleshed fish that is great to serve The Progeny, as it definitely tastes like fish, but not too much like fish. The apricot salsa requires a few minutes of chopping, but it's nothing Dad can't handle. Just remember Dad's Official Cooking Mantra #14—*If I'm cooking in the kitchen, I don't have to be out cleaning the garage.*

Serves 4

Ingredients

½ cup finely chopped dried apricots

½ cup red or yellow bell pepper, stemmed, seeded, and cut into 1-inch pieces

⅓ cup chopped scallions, green parts only

1 tablespoon minced fresh ginger

2 cloves garlic, minced

2 tablespoons fresh lemon juice

1 teaspoon brown sugar

1 teaspoon hot sauce

½ teaspoon salt

1 tablespoon Thai chili paste

4 grouper fillets (about 6 ounces each)

Spray cooking oil

→ **Combine** the apricots, bell pepper, scallions, ginger, garlic, lemon juice, brown sugar, hot sauce, and salt in a medium bowl. Set aside.

Prepare enough coals for a hot charcoal fire, or preheat your gas grill on high for 10 minutes with the lid closed.

While the grill is heating up, apply a thin layer of Thai chili paste to both sides of the fillets.

When the coals are ready or the gas grill is hot, liberally spray one side of each fillet with cooking oil. Place on the grate, oiled side down, and grill for 4 minutes, until the skin is golden brown and a crust has formed. Spray the top of each fillet with more cooking oil and gently turn them over. Grill for 4 to 5 minutes more, until the center is just cooked through. Transfer to a serving platter and top with apricot salsa.

Miso-Ginger Marinated Grilled Salmon

You might be wondering, "Three grilled salmon recipes?" (counting the super-fast Grilled Lemon Rosemary Salmon in Foil on page 187). But here's the thing—salmon on the grill is so easy and so improbably good that you should have as many reasons as possible to make it. This one surges with flavor from the miso paste, the procuring of which might take you to heretofore unfrequented markets, like an Asian grocery. Good. See what else is around. Grab some black sesame seeds, for instance, which you can sprinkle on any number of dishes and, with just a flick of the wrist, instantly make them more exotic. **Serves 4**

Ingredients

¼ cup white miso (fermented soybean paste)

¼ cup mirin rice wine

2 tablespoons unseasoned rice vinegar

2 to 3 tablespoons soy sauce

2 tablespoons minced scallion, green parts only

2 tablespoons finely chopped fresh ginger

2 teaspoons sesame oil

4 salmon fillets (8 ounces each)

Spray cooking oil

→ **Whisk** together the miso, mirin, vinegar, soy sauce, scallion, ginger, and sesame oil in a small bowl. Place the salmon on a platter and coat with the marinade. Cover and refrigerate for at least 1 hour and up to 4 hours.

Prepare enough coals for a hot charcoal fire, or preheat your gas grill on high for 10 minutes with the lid closed.

When the coals are ready or the gas grill is hot, liberally spray the skin side of each salmon fillet with cooking oil. Place on the grate, skin side down, and grill for 5 minutes, until the skin is golden brown and a crust has formed. Spray the top of each fillet with more cooking oil and gently turn over. Grill for 4 to 5 minutes more, until the center is just cooked through and is no longer pink.

Transfer the salmon fillets to a platter and serve immediately.

Salmon with Mango Salsa

Don't be afraid of mangoes. I admit they don't peel as easily as an orange and are possessed of an oddly shaped and prudish pit that seems to defy your knife's advances. But once you've negotiated the sweet flesh from a few mangoes, you'll be hooked and The Progeny will totally dig the sweet and tangy addition to their grilled salmon.

Serves 4

Ingredients

3 tablespoons fresh lime juice

½ cup chopped fresh cilantro

1 small red onion, finely chopped

1 mango, peeled, pitted, and coarsely chopped (see instructions below)

1 red bell pepper, stemmed, seeded, and finely chopped

½ teaspoon chili powder

½ teaspoon salt

Dash of hot sauce

4 salmon fillets (6 ounces each)

Spray cooking oil

→ **In** a medium bowl, combine the lime juice, cilantro, red onion, mango, bell pepper, chili powder, salt, and hot sauce. Toss gently and set aside.

Prepare enough coals for a hot charcoal fire, or preheat your gas grill on high for 10 minutes with the lid closed.

While the grill is hot, liberally spray the skin side of each salmon fillet with cooking oil. Place salmon fillets on grill, skin side down, and grill for 5 minutes, until the skin is golden brown and a crust has formed. Spray the top of each fillet with more cooking oil and gently turn over. Grill for 4 to 5 minutes more, until the center is just cooked through.

Transfer the salmon to individual plates, top with several spoonfuls of the mango salsa, and serve.

Note: *Choose a mango with a fruity aroma, one that yields slightly to pressure from your thumb. It will ripen further while sitting on your counter. As with most stone fruit, you can speed up the ripening process by sticking the fruit in a paper bag. The following procedure will make perfect sense once you do it. To peel the mango, hold it in place on the cutting board lengthwise and use a serrated knife to slice off the flesh from both sides of the pit. If you encounter the pit as you slice, you may have to finesse the knife a bit to avoid it. Score the flesh by running the knife tip up to the skin in sections about ½ inch apart. Then do the same crosswise. Press the skin inward, in a sense turning the mango half inside out, causing the scored sections to protrude. Trim these off and repeat with the other side. Trim off the remaining slivers attached to the narrow end of the pit and trim off the skin. The mango is now ready to be served or chopped more finely, if necessary.*

Salmon with Mango Salsa

Chicago-Style Hot Dogs

Classic Panini

Foolproof Burger

Barbecued Game Hens "Under the Brick"

Grilled Pizza with Pepperoni & Mushrooms

Grilled Porterhouse

Grilled Snapper Tacos

Grilled Sweet Potatoes

Honey-Glazed Spare Ribs

Roasted Corn with Chipotle Butter

Prosciutto-Wrapped Grilled Asparagus

Savory Roast Beef Sandwiches

Shrimp & Smoked Sausage Kabobs

Steak Tacos

Striped Bass Fillets with Tomato Corn Relish

Striped Bass Fillets with Tomato & Corn Relish

A perfect topping for a perfect fish that works great on the grill. Striped bass is a subtly flavored white–fleshed fish that tastes, well, a lot like fish. It really comes alive when cooked on the grill. Make sure the relish is at room temperature before serving.

Serves 4

Ingredients

1 pound cherry tomatoes, cut in half

1 small red onion, peeled, halved lengthwise, and cut into thin slices

One 6-ounce can corn kernels packed in water, drained well

One 4-ounce jar roasted red peppers, drained well and cut into medium dice

¼ cup coarsely chopped flat-leaf parsley

¼ cup coarsely chopped fresh basil leaves

2 tablespoons finely chopped fresh mint

2½ tablespoons fresh lemon juice

Freshly ground black pepper

¼ cup extra virgin olive oil

4 striped bass fillets (6 ounces each)

Salt

Spray cooking oil

→ **In** a medium bowl, combine the tomatoes, onion, corn, roasted peppers, parsley, basil, mint, lemon juice, pepper to taste, and olive oil. Toss gently and set aside, or cover and refrigerate for up to 4 hours.

Prepare enough coals for a hot charcoal fire, or preheat your gas grill on high for 10 minutes with the lid closed.

Season both sides of the striped bass fillets with salt and pepper to taste.

When the coals are ready or the gas grill is hot, spray the skin side of the fillets liberally with cooking oil and place them skin side down on the grill. Grill the fillets for 4 minutes, until the skin is golden brown and a crust has formed. Spray the fillets again with oil, turn, and grill for 3 to 4 minutes more, until they are just cooked through.

Transfer the striped bass fillets to individual plates, top with several spoonfuls of the tomato-corn relish, and serve.

Grilled Snapper Tacos

Grilled fish tacos are a staple in Southern California. Rather than the usual salsa that accompanies meat–filled tacos, those filled with fish get topped with finely chopped sweet onion and fresh cilantro and a squeeze of fresh lime. Once you taste them, you'll know why. There's nothing better to eat while you're sitting on a bench looking out over the water in Laguna. Just make sure you're far enough away from the beach volleyball game to avoid getting flying sand in your taco. **Makes 12 tacos**

Ingredients

12 corn tortillas

1 medium sweet onion, finely chopped

1 bunch cilantro, finely chopped

¼ cup fresh lime juice

Salt and freshly ground black pepper

2 pounds red snapper fillets

2 teaspoons chili powder

2 teaspoons paprika

2 teaspoons dried oregano

Spray cooking oil

4 limes, quartered, for serving

Hot sauce, for serving

→ **Wrap** the tortillas in aluminum foil, in 3 packages of 4 tortillas each, and set aside.

In a medium bowl, mix together the chopped onion, cilantro, and lime juice. Season with salt and pepper to taste. Set aside, or cover and refrigerate for up to 4 hours.

Prepare enough coals for a hot charcoal fire, or preheat your gas grill on high for 10 minutes with the lid closed.

While the grill is heating up, season the tops of the snapper fillets with the chili powder, paprika, oregano, and a sprinkling of salt and pepper. Place the tortilla packages in the oven and set it at 250°F. Warm for up to 30 minutes.

When the coals are ready or the gas grill is hot, liberally spray the skin side of each snapper fillet with cooking oil. Place on the grate, skin side down, and grill for 4 minutes, until the skin is golden brown and a crust has formed. Spray the top of each fillet with more cooking oil and gently turn them over. Grill for 4 to 5 minutes more, until the center is just cooked through.

Transfer the snapper fillets to a cutting board, and cut them into quarters. Put on a serving table with the warm tortillas, onion-cilantro mixture, quartered limes, and hot sauce, and let people assemble their own tacos.

Shrimp & Smoked Sausage Kabobs

You can throw these kabobs together in less time than it takes to lace up a pair of The Progeny's ice skates (something I'm glad I'll never have to do again). After only a few minutes on the grill, you'll have a fast and easy main course. **Serves 4**

Ingredients

8 bamboo skewers

1 pound large shrimp (26–30 size), peeled and deveined

1 pound smoked sausage, cut into ¾-inch rounds

1 red bell pepper, stemmed, seeded, and cut into roughly 1-inch squares

Spray cooking oil

2 tablespoons extra virgin olive oil

Salt and freshly ground black pepper

➜ **One** hour before grilling, soak the bamboo skewers in warm water.

Prepare enough coals for a hot charcoal fire, or preheat your gas grill on high for 10 minutes with the lid closed.

While the coals are heating up, thread the shrimp, smoked sausage, and red pepper squares onto the skewers, making sure not to crowd them too closely.

When the coals are ready or the gas grill is hot, spray the kabobs liberally with cooking oil and place them on the grill. Cook for 3 minutes. Spray the kabobs again with oil, turn, and grill for 2 to 3 minutes more, until the shrimp are just cooked through.

Transfer the skewers to a platter. Drizzle with the olive oil and season to taste with salt and pepper. Serve immediately.

Mediterranean Jumbo Shrimp

I like that The Progeny think of me as someone who knows how to combine spices so they work together in harmony. I'm like an ancient alchemist, conjuring up obscure potions, working my magic. I leave the different spice jars on the counter so they can see how many went into a dish like this. Other dads on the block might know how to seal their own driveway or rebuild the clutch on a vintage GTO. But I am the dad who is intimate with the secrets of ground coriander and understands the mysterious dark arts of allspice. I have used these powers to create this grilled shrimp recipe, which is anything but ordinary. **Serves 4**

Ingredients

4 long bamboo skewers

1 teaspoon ground cinnamon

1 teaspoon ground cumin

1 teaspoon ground coriander

1 teaspoon paprika

1 teaspoon ground ginger

½ teaspoon ground allspice

½ teaspoon cayenne pepper

1 teaspoon salt

16 jumbo shrimp (10–16 size), peeled and deveined

¼ cup extra virgin olive oil

1 cup chopped fresh cilantro

1 tablespoon finely chopped garlic

Spray cooking oil

Orange wedges, for serving

→ **One** hour before grilling, soak the bamboo skewers in warm water.

In a small bowl, combine the cinnamon, cumin, coriander, paprika, ginger, allspice, cayenne, and salt.

Place the shrimp in a large bowl and sprinkle with the spice mixture. Add the olive oil, cilantro, and garlic and mix together so the shrimp are evenly coated. Refrigerate the shrimp until ready to use, up to 1 hour.

Prepare enough coals for a hot charcoal fire, or preheat your gas grill on high for 10 minutes with the lid closed.

While the coals are heating up, thread the shrimp onto the skewers, making sure not to crowd them.

When the coals are ready or the gas grill is hot, spray the shrimp on both sides with cooking oil and grill them for 3 minutes. Turn and grill for 3 to 4 minutes more, until they are just cooked through.

Transfer the skewers to a platter and serve with the orange wedges.

Grilled Lobster Tails

Every once in a while, the stars align and you will find yourself having dinner with one of The Progeny. Perhaps Mom is off visiting family and the other kids are on a school trip, so it's just you and one of your kids. It's a rare occurrence, so do something special, like grill up these obscenely good lobster tails. Simply lay them on the grill, smother the succulent meat with butter and basil and a dusting of sea salt, and dig in. And even though it may be a while before you're alone together again, resist the impulse to earnestly gaze across the table at your kid and ask them, "So how are you *really*?" **Serves 2**

Ingredients

Two 8-ounce lobster tails

1 tablespoon extra-virgin olive oil

4 tablespoons (½ stick) butter

¼ cup chopped fresh basil

Sea salt

→ **Using** kitchen scissors, butterfly the lobster tails by laying them shell-side down on the counter and cutting through the middle of the tail but not through the back shell. Bend the lobster tail back to open up the meat—the shell should crack but hold together.

Prepare enough coals for a medium-hot charcoal fire, or preheat your gas grill on medium-high for 10 minutes with the lid closed.

When the coals are ready or the gas grill is hot, brush the lobster meat with the olive oil. Place on the grill flesh-side down, pushing down just a bit. Cook for 5 minutes. Turn and cook about 5 minutes more until the meat is opaque.

While the lobster is cooking, put the butter and basil in a small saucepan and let it melt on the outer edge of the grill.

When the lobsters are done, transfer to a platter and spoon the warm butter over them. Sprinkle with sea salt and serve.

BURGERS, DOGS & BRATS

Fig. 8: *Foolproof Burger*

For Dad, it's all about the burger. It's the perfect marriage of meat and heat. The burger does not disappoint.

It is low maintenance. Its needs are simple. It requires no fancy, high-fashion designer bread. No trendy sauces. No expensive condiments it just can't be seen in school without. It doesn't miss curfew. It doesn't require cajoling or threatening in order to reveal its true self. The burger is not in a chat room when it should be doing algebra homework.

The burger is self-sufficient. It requires little attention while cooking. It sits on the grill until it needs turning. When it's done, you separate the bun, you put the burger between the two halves along with some lettuce and tomato—or not—and some ketchup and, perhaps, some mustard as well. And that's it.

When you serve burgers, your family eats happily.

There is nothing vague or enigmatic about the burger. Men are from Mars—burgers are from Mars. What more could a dad want?

Burger Basics

Meat

Ground round (15 percent fat) makes for a juicy but not overwhelmingly fatty burger. Ground chuck (20 percent fat) also works. Ground sirloin (10 percent fat) makes a leaner but slightly less satisfying burger. Avoid frozen burger patties, as their only purpose is as a meat-flavored ketchup delivery system.

Size

Burger size matters. Too big and the outside burns before the inside is cooked. Too thin and it will cook through before it gets a chance to be medium-rare. The optimum size is 6 ounces of meat shaped into a patty about ¾-inch thick and 4 inches across. This means you need 1½ pounds of meat to make 4 burgers.

Cooking

Cooking a burger is as easy as, well, cooking a burger.

1. Don't mash the patty—assemble the meat into a hamburger shape by handling it as little as possible. The less tightly the meat is packed, the juicier the results.

2. Don't pat the burgers while they are cooking. Just leave them alone. They know what to do. Keep your eye on the clock and turn them only once. A happy spatula makes for a sad burger.

3. If you are making cheeseburgers, get the cheese on as soon as you turn the burgers—you don't want to have to sacrifice medium-rareness to get the cheese melted.

4. Salt both sides just before grilling—do not mix the salt into the meat, which will overwhelm the essential burger flavor.

5. Have the buns and condiments ready, the drinks chilled, and the table set before you put the burgers on the heat. That way, when the burgers are at their peak, you have everything set to go.

6. Bun to meat ratio: The bun should not overwhelm the burger. Some people like their burgers on rolls the size of monster truck tires. Personally, I think a classic hamburger roll is the perfect size, and their nondescript flavor doesn't compete with the meat.

Foolproof Burgers

"Foolproof," of course, only if you don't screw it up. The key is to be patient. Leave the burgers alone and let the fire do its magic. Don't be impetuous with your spatula, furtively patting the patties as though you're on a second date in junior high. Only when the burgers are done do you get to interact with them. But when they *are* done, you need to be decisive and get them off the grill. Remember, it is better to discreetly cut into one of the burgers to see if they are medium-rare (you can eat that one yourself) than to leave them on the grill for too long. **Makes 4 burgers**

Ingredients

1½ pounds ground round

Salt

4 classic hamburger buns

Condiments of your choice, for serving

→ **Shape** the meat into four 6-ounce burgers, each about ¾ inch thick and 4 inches across.

Prepare enough coals for a hot charcoal fire, or preheat your gas grill on high for 10 minutes with the lid closed.

When the coals are ready or the gas grill is hot, sprinkle the burgers with salt to taste and grill them for 8 to 9 minutes, turning once, until they are medium-rare.

Transfer to a bun. Add condiments and serve.

Lamb Burgers

Melted into the meat, the feta loses its overbearing presence and provides a subtle tanginess that enhances the lamb. I like to prepare these lamb burgers for the adults when we are having another family for a barbecue (they take about 1 minute longer to cook). But The Progeny should also try them to experience the different flavors. And if they are ever presumptuous enough to wonder why you didn't just make them regular burgers, inform them politely that they will "thank you later."

Makes 4 burgers

Ingredients

1½ pounds ground lamb

1 egg

¼ cup bread crumbs

4 ounces feta cheese, crumbled into pea-sized pieces

2 tablespoons pine nuts

8 kalamata olives (a scant ¼ cup), pitted and chopped

3 tablespoons finely chopped fresh garlic

1 teaspoon curry powder

1 tablespoon chopped fresh oregano, or 1 teaspoon dried

1 teaspoon salt

½ teaspoon ground nutmeg

½ teaspoon cayenne pepper

4 pita breads

Shredded lettuce, for serving

Chopped tomato, for serving

Cumin-Spiced Yogurt Dressing (recipe on facing page), for serving

→ **Place** the ground lamb in a large bowl and add the egg, bread crumbs, feta, pine nuts, olives, garlic, curry powder, oregano, salt, nutmeg, and cayenne, and gently mix together until just combined. Shape the meat into 4 burgers about ¾ inch thick and 4½ inches across.

Prepare enough coals for a hot charcoal fire, or preheat your gas grill on high for 10 minutes with the lid closed.

When the coals are ready or the gas grill is hot, grill the lamb burgers for 9 to 10 minutes, turning once, until they are medium.

Transfer the burgers to the pitas. Top with lettuce and tomato and serve with the yogurt dressing.

Cumin-Spiced Yogurt Dressing

This sauce cools and refreshes as it adds a bit more complexity to the burger with a hint of cumin.

Makes about 1 cup

Ingredients

1 cup plain yogurt

1 tablespoon fresh lemon juice

1 teaspoon ground cumin

½ teaspoon curry powder

½ teaspoon ground ginger

½ teaspoon salt

→ **Mix** all of the ingredients together in a small bowl. Add more salt if needed. Keep refrigerated until ready to use. The dressing can be made up to 4 days in advance.

POP CULTURE

Do I Really Have to Use a Food Processor?

HOW, YOU MAY BE WONDERING, did we get from the spacious idyll of the backyard and the comforting, manly presence of the grill to the more suspect domain of the kitchen counter and the unsettling specter of the food processor? What gives?

In *Apocalypse Now*, Colonel Kilgore shouted the famous line, "Charlie don't surf!"

You say, *Dad don't process!*

Well, I say, *get over it.*

Using a food processor is no harder than putting air in your tires (you know how to do that, don't you?). You set the processor bowl on the motor unit. You fit in the metal blade. You add the stuff. You put on the lid. You pulse until it's chopped the way you want it. You use a rubber spatula and get the chopped mixture out.

That's it.

For this book, you don't need to use the processor for anything other than chopping. That means you'll employ only the steel blade, so you don't need to worry about any of the oddly shaped attachments that look like medieval torture devices. Once you process with the processor a few times, you will understand. This is a machine that makes you look good. You will give one to your friend for his birthday. You will write odes to it. It won't let you down. I promise.

(well, only for chopping)

Cajun Turkey Burgers

Turkey burgers are what you might compare something to if you wanted to emphasize its ineluctable banality, as in "That's as dry and dull and sad as, well, as a *turkey burger*." But far from having a paucity of flavor, these turkey burgers are actually *good*. Really good. They are juicy and daring, and the inclusion of the sausage gives them an extra bit of exhilaration. Throwing some hickory chips on the coals for a hint of smokiness also doesn't hurt (see the note at the end of the recipe). Be sure to give the patties a good spray of oil before turning to keep them from sticking to the grate.

Makes 4 burgers

Ingredients

1 pound ground turkey

8 ounces Cajun-style smoked chicken sausages, cut into ¼-inch dice

1 large egg, lightly beaten

2 scallions, green parts only, finely chopped

One 2-ounce can diced green chiles

One 4-ounce jar roasted red peppers, drained and finely chopped

3 tablespoons finely chopped fresh garlic

1 tablespoon chili powder

½ teaspoon salt

Freshly ground black pepper

Spray cooking oil

4 classic hamburger rolls

Chili sauce, for serving

Lettuce leaves and thinly sliced red onion, for serving

→ **Place** the ground turkey in a medium bowl. Add the sausage, egg, scallions, green chiles, roasted peppers, garlic, chili powder, salt, and pepper to taste. Gently mix together until just combined. Shape the meat into 4 burgers about ¾ inch thick and 4½ inches across and refrigerate until ready to use.

Prepare enough coals for a medium-hot charcoal fire, or preheat your gas grill on medium-high for 10 minutes with the lid closed.

When the coals are ready or the gas grill is hot, spray one side of the burgers with cooking oil.

Place on the grate, oiled side down, and grill for 6 minutes. Spray the tops of the burgers, turn, and cook for 5 to 6 minutes more, until the center is no longer pink.

Transfer immediately to the buns. Top with chili sauce, lettuce, and red onion and serve.

Note: *If you want to add a hint of hickory smoke, at least 1 hour before grilling, soak 1 cup of wood chips in water to cover. When the coals are ready, lift the chips from the water and scatter them over the coals. Immediately proceed with the grilling.*

Tuna Burgers

A tuna burger may sound like an oxymoron, but it is actually a sublime marriage of flavors—a charred, smoky crust outside with a soft, exotic, Asian-inspired interior. Because tuna burgers are best served medium-rare, you want to get your tuna from a reputable fish store where you know it is fresh and has been stored properly.

Makes 4 burgers

Ingredients

1½ **pounds fresh tuna steak**

2 **cloves garlic, chopped**

2 **tablespoons finely chopped fresh ginger**

3 **tablespoons soy sauce**

2 **scallions, green parts only, chopped**

½ **small red bell pepper, stemmed, seeded, and finely chopped**

2 **teaspoons sesame oil**

1 **teaspoon salt**

½ **teaspoon cayenne pepper**

Spray cooking oil

4 **sesame kaiser rolls, split**

Mango chutney and spicy Chinese mustard, for serving

4 **leaves red-leaf lettuce, for serving**

→ **Cube** the tuna into 1-inch pieces and place in the bowl of a food processor fitted with a steel blade. Pulse until the tuna is coarsely ground, about the consistency of hamburger.

Transfer the tuna to a bowl and mix in the garlic, ginger, soy sauce, scallions, bell pepper, sesame oil, salt, and cayenne pepper until well combined.

Form 4 patties, about 1½ inches thick.

Prepare enough coals for a medium-hot charcoal fire, or preheat your gas grill on medium-high for 10 minutes with the lid closed.

When the coals are ready or the gas grill is hot, spray one side of the tuna burgers with cooking oil. Place on the grate, oiled side down, and grill for 4 minutes. Spray the tops of the burgers with oil, turn, and cook for 3 to 4 minutes more for medium-rare.

Transfer the tuna burgers to the bottom halves of the rolls and top with either the mango chutney or the hot mustard or both. Add the lettuce and the tops of the rolls and serve.

Dad Burgers

Around my house these are called Dad Burgers because I'm the only one allowed to make them. Each burger features a surprise filling secreted away in the center. Sometimes they are all the same. Sometimes each one is different. The thing about Dad Burgers is that you never know exactly what you're going to get.

Makes 4 burgers

Ingredients

6 slices bacon

1½ pounds ground round

4 ounces Cheddar cheese, grated

Salt

4 classic hamburger buns

Condiments of your choice, for serving

→ **Place** a skillet over medium-high heat. When it is hot, add the bacon slices and cook until lightly browned, about 4 minutes. Turn and cook for about 4 minutes more. Transfer the bacon to a paper towel–lined plate and pat gently to remove the excess fat. When the bacon slices are cool enough to handle, break them up into small, cornflake–sized pieces and set aside.

To make the burgers, divide the meat into 8 roughly equal portions. Press out half of each portion into a flat round about 4½ inches across. Place about a tablespoon of chopped bacon on the center of 4 of the patties, being sure to keep about a half-inch rim around it. Place one-fourth of the grated cheese on top of the bacon. Arrange a second patty of meat over the bacon and cheese, and press the edges together so they are nicely sealed.

Prepare enough coals for a hot charcoal fire, or preheat your gas grill on high for 10 minutes with the lid closed.

When the coals are ready or the gas grill is hot, sprinkle the burgers with salt and grill them for 8 to 9 minutes, turning once, until they are medium-rare.

Transfer to a bun. Add condiments and serve.

Other favorite Dad Burger combos:
Sautéed mushrooms and Gruyère cheese
Chopped ham and Taleggio cheese
Hot capicolla and provolone
Blue cheese and more blue cheese

Mexican Chicken Burgers

The Progeny often enjoy contemplating grand philosophical conundrums. *God* spelled backward is *Dog*. If a tree falls in the forest, and no one is around to hear it, does it really make a sound? And, most profound of all, whether a burger not served on a bun can actually be called a burger. There is no better occasion to argue this weighty matter than with a plate of tortilla chips topped with guacamole, salsa, and one of these really tasty patties (I'll use this more neutral nomenclature until you resolve the issue for yourselves). **Makes 4 patties**

Ingredients

1½ pounds ground chicken

½ cup chopped fresh cilantro

6 scallions, green parts only, finely chopped

2 cloves garlic, crushed

2 teaspoons chili powder

1 tablespoon ground cumin

1 teaspoon salt

½ cup unseasoned bread crumbs

1 egg, lightly beaten

One 1-pound bag tortilla chips

½ head romaine lettuce, shredded

One 15-ounce can refried beans

Spray cooking oil

4 slices sharp Cheddar cheese

1 medium red onion, finely chopped

One 12-ounce jar salsa

1 cup Guacamole (page 205)

⅓ cup sour cream

→ **In** a large bowl, mix together the chicken, ¼ cup of the cilantro, the scallions, garlic, chili powder, cumin, salt, bread crumbs, and egg until well combined (it's probably best to use your hands for this). Shape the mixture into 4 patties about ¾ inch thick and 4½ inches across. Place the patties on a platter, cover, and refrigerate for up to 12 hours, until ready to use.

Prepare enough coals for a medium-hot charcoal fire, or preheat your gas grill on medium-high for 10 minutes with the lid closed.

While the grill is heating up, arrange the tortilla chips around the edges of 4 dinner plates. Pile the lettuce in the center. Set these aside. Put the refried beans into a small saucepan.

When the coals are ready or the gas grill is hot, spray one side of the patties with cooking oil. Place them on the grate, oiled side down, and grill for 6 minutes. Spray the tops of the burgers, turn, and lay a slice of Cheddar over each patty. Grill 5 to 6 minutes more, until the center is no longer pink. During the last few minutes of cooking, set the saucepan with the refried beans in a corner of the grill. Stir occasionally until the beans are heated through.

Transfer each patty to a dinner plate, nestling it gently on the bed of lettuce. Top the patty with a few tablespoons of refried beans, followed by some chopped onions, salsa, guacamole, and sour cream. Garnish with the remaining cilantro and serve.

The Hot Dog

There are three basic hot dog motifs:

1. The mild frank topped with a vigorous and, often, idiosyncratic array of toppings.

2. The spicy, flavorful dog served simply, perhaps with just a hint of mustard and/or a toupee of kraut.

3. The spicy, flavorful dog topped with a vigorous and, often, idiosyncratic array of toppings.

Regional tastes play with these recipes, and, once they are established, the locals adhere to them with a frenzied devotion.

Types of Hot Dogs

There really is a difference between brands. Some are bland, some have abundant flavor. Some are smoked, some not. I won't advise you on which dogs to purchase, other than to say what could be more fun than gathering several different brands, cooking them up, and having a hot dog taste test with The Progeny. The goal—to find the perfect one. You could even do this several times—once a week, say, so you really feel confident with your assessments. I will assert, however, that if you live in the vicinity of a butcher or gourmet shop that makes their own hot dogs and sausages, you should try every-thing they have, even if the hot dogs wear a hue that may, at first, seem un–hot-dog-like—that probably just means they have more flavor.

Cooking the Dog

A natural casing makes for a perfect crispy hot dog, but only if you don't cook it too much, causing the skin to burst and, consequently, the flavor to escape. Medium heat is essential for proper hot dog cooking. Remember, the meat inside is already seasoned. Grilling just enhances this flavor. Slower heat will cook the dogs through, give the outside a touch of charred flavor, but allow the juicy interior to stay intact. Some people make surgical slits in their dogs to help the inside cook faster. I hope I don't have to work too hard to dissuade you from this practice.

Chicago-Style Hot Dogs

Chicagoans are serious about their hot dogs. Mike Royko, the legendary *Tribune* reporter, respected people's "right to put mayo or chocolate syrup or toenail clippings or cat hair on their hot dog," but if they deviated even slightly from the officially sanctioned condiments, they were not eating a Chicago hot dog. Chicagoans hold fiercely to the ritual of their assembly, much like superstitious pitchers who never step on the chalk lines on their way to and from the dugout. Especially taboo is ketchup. Many Windy City dog emporiums don't even stock it. Chicago dogs are usually boiled or steamed, though some places grill them, in which case they are identified as "chardogs." But it's the idiosyncratic assemblage of toppings that makes this hot dog distinct. And unless you include them all—the relish *and* the pickle wedge—you have no claim to having consumed a true Chicago dog. **Makes 8 hot dogs**

Ingredients

1 medium sweet onion, finely chopped

2 Roma tomatoes, seeded and diced

Thinly sliced sport or banana peppers (optional)

Yellow mustard

Green relish

4 thin pickle wedges

Dash celery salt

8 hot dog buns

8 all-beef, natural-casing Vienna hot dogs

→ **Put** the chopped onion, tomatoes, and optional sport or banana peppers in small bowls and arrange them on a serving table, along with the mustard, relish, pickle wedges, celery salt, and buns.

Prepare enough coals for a medium charcoal fire, or preheat your gas grill on medium for 10 minutes with the lid closed.

When the coals are ready or the gas grill is hot, grill the hot dogs for 7 minutes, turning regularly to keep them from excessive charring.

Place the grilled hot dogs on a platter and set them on the serving table with the buns and condiments, and get busy.

A Hot Dog Atlas

CHEESE CONEY

Topped with: Cincinnati chili, mustard, diced onion, and shredded mild Cheddar cheese

Natural Habitat: Cincinnati

LA (LOWER ALABAMA) DOG

Topped with: Ketchup, mustard, chili, sauerkraut, and pickles

Natural Habitat: Alabama, New Orleans during Mardi Gras

SONORA HOT DOG

Topped with: Wrapped in mesquite-smoked bacon and topped with chopped tomatoes, onions, shredded cheese, tomatillo salsa and/or red chili sauce, pinto beans, mayonnaise, ketchup, and/or mustard

Natural Habitat: Tucson, Metro Phoenix, and Sonora, Mexico

SCRAMBLED DOG

Topped with: Mustard, ketchup, a spicy chili made with beans and chunks of diced raw onion, pickles, and oyster crackers; served in a banana split bowl and eaten by cowards with a knife and fork

Natural Habitat: Georgia

CONEY ISLAND

Topped with: All-meat, beanless chili, diced yellow onion, and yellow mustard

Natural Habitat: Lower Michigan

POTATO DOG

Topped with: Diced, stewed potatoes and brown mustard and sometimes grilled onions and peppers, in which case it bears the moniker Italian Hot Dog

Natural Habitat: New Jersey

CAROLINA DOG

Topped with: Chili, coleslaw, mustard, and onions

Natural Habitat: North and South Carolina

Brats

Brats come in basically one shape and size but many different flavors. Butchers in Wisconsin, the heart of brat country, particularly pride themselves on the quality and variety of their sausages and vie to maintain their loyal fans. As with hot dogs, you must cook brats over a medium fire. Think of them the way you would if you were in the batter's box facing Nolan Ryan—you have to lay off the high heat. So if you are grilling burgers at the same time, prepare enough coals for a two-tiered fire, keeping the brats cozied up on the medium side of the grill.

Unlike hot dogs, brats are usually served with only a modicum of adornment. True brat lovers let the brats do most of the work. The classic Sheboygan (Wisconsin) "double with the works" is topped only with pickles, ketchup, onions, and stone-ground mustard—hardly much "works" compared with some of the more baroque regional hot dog concoctions. Sauerkraut is also popular, especially in the parking lot of Lambeau Field before, during, and after Packers games, where brats are transferred directly from the grill to a holding pen, which is a saucepan of warm kraut, before being placed on the buns.

More problematic than the appropriate toppings for brats are the buns. Regular hot dog buns are not quite ample enough. The brats look like teenagers who went through puberty and are still stuck in last year's pants. Kaiser rolls are the choice of many, especially if they are serving the traditional "double stack." If not, one brat in a round roll only serves to allow the brat to extrude immodestly from the roll's perimeter. You may have to look for a local bakery or specialty food shop that carries a small torpedo roll that will comfortably house your brats. In Wisconsin, of course, bakeries make a special rye-flour roll, slightly crusty on the outside, soft on the inside, that is the perfect shape for a brat.

Classic Grilled Brats

It's not just the manly Wisconsin men who down these double brats. It's how all Wis-consinites muster the resilience to get through the long winters. The traditional way to arrange the pair of brats on the bun is not, as you might imagine, discreetly side by side, à la Doris Day and Rock Hudson in *Pillow Talk*, but more in the spirit of William Hurt and Kathleen Turner on the living room floor in *Body Heat*. **Serves 6**

Ingredients

1 cup finely chopped onions

One 6-ounce jar sliced dill pickles

Bavarian or other spicy brown mustard

Ketchup

6 hard rolls, halved and well buttered

12 bratwurst

→ **Ready** the onions, pickles, mustard, ketchup, and rolls so they are set to go when the brats come off the grill.

Prepare enough coals for a medium charcoal fire, or preheat your gas grill on medium for 10 minutes with the lid closed.

When the coals are ready or the gas grill is hot, grill the bratwurst for 10 to 12 minutes, turning occasionally, until they are cooked through and dark golden brown.

Transfer the cooked brats to a cutting board, cut them almost all the way through lengthwise, and open them up like a book. Stack a pair of brats on each roll and let everyone add whatever accompaniments they desire.

Brats with Cherries & Bacon

If you've been having sleepless nights because The Progeny have been clamoring incessantly for a brat stuffed with grilled fruit and the added punch of a swath of smoked bacon, you can finally breathe a sigh of relief. This recipe is the answer. Not only will it satisfy their cravings, but it's a perfect dish to get the kids involved. Make an assembly line at the prep counter—you can start by slitting open the brats and then passing them down to the cherry stuffing station and finally one more pass for the bacon wrap. When you pull these off the grill, the crispy bacon and warm sweetness of the cherries make it a truly special treat (have I said that too many times already?). **Makes 8 bratwurst**

Ingredients

8 sweet, unsmoked bratwurst

8 ounces pitted cherries, thawed if frozen

16 slices bacon

8 sandwich rolls

Dijon-style mustard, for serving

→ **Use** a serrated knife to cut the bratwurst lengthwise, cutting halfway through. Stuff the cherries inside the opening, 4 or 5 for each sausage. Wrap 2 slices of bacon around each sausage, keeping the cherries in place.

Prepare enough coals for a medium charcoal fire, or preheat your gas grill on medium for 10 minutes with the lid closed.

When the coals are ready or the gas grill is hot, grill the cherry-stuffed brats for 10 to 12 minutes, turning occasionally, until they are cooked through and the bacon is a dark, golden brown.

Transfer the cooked brats to a platter and serve with the rolls and mustard.

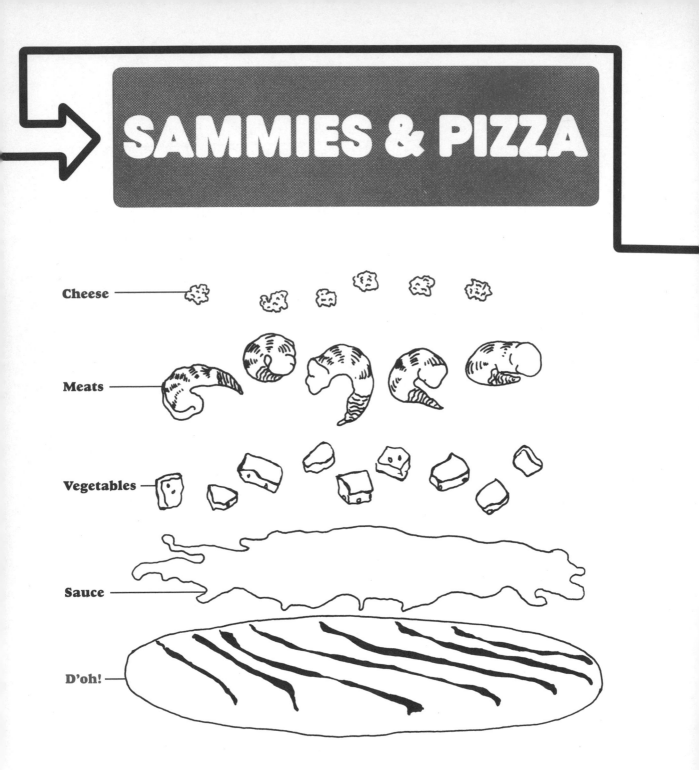

Cheese

Meats

Vegetables

Sauce

D'oh!

Fig. 9: *Grilled Pizza with Shrimp & Feta*

09

I'm thinking of the drawing of that iconic fifties guy in the barbecue apron, slightly overfed, toque flopping somewhat buffoonishly to the side, proudly bearing a carving fork in one hand and effusively displaying a platter of steak in the other.

That jolly Apron Guy could probably not conceive of the idea that a new generation of men is cooking up all kinds of food on their grills. Never mind the odd cuts of meat, like short ribs and hanger steaks; he could probably wrap his mind around that. But fish?? And vegetables?? Preposterous.

And Apron Guy would be even more apoplectic at the sight of a pizza cooking peacefully right in the center of his grill. Or panini, which are really hypnotically good grilled cheese sandwiches, or the round aluminum space–discs of foil-wrapped quesadillas lingering on the heat just long enough to get the cheese warm so it melts luxuriously into the filling.

These ideas for a special lunch or a more casual dinner will allow you to add some new notches on your grill handles.

Oh, and by the way, only on rare occasions do men display the bib portion of their aprons. Otherwise, that part is tucked behind the skirt and, once the apron is tied, remains completely hidden from view.

Classic Panini

This is more than just a glorified grilled cheese sandwich. The combination of prosciutto and pesto elevates it to new heights, like when Hendrix took the very ordinary midtempo R&B song "Hey Joe," slowed it way down, and gradually built up his vocals to a cathartic confession capped by a searing guitar solo. I've prepped a 4-foot stack of these panini, the rickety tower looking like something out of a Dr. Seuss book, and then grilled them off six at a time to feed The Progeny and a flock of their friends. Needless to say, everyone was happy. **Makes 4 panini**

Ingredients

4 pieces focaccia, sliced in half horizontally

Olive oil, for brushing

2 ounces jarred sun-dried tomato pesto

8 ounces fontina cheese, sliced

8 thin slices prosciutto

2 bricks wrapped in foil, or other suitable weight

➔ **Brush** the outside of each focaccia slice with olive oil. Lightly brush the inside of one half of the focaccia with olive oil. Spread a thin layer of the sun-dried tomato pesto over the other half.

On the bottom half of each sandwich, place 1 slice of cheese, 2 slices of prosciutto, and then 1 more slice of cheese. Top with the remaining focaccia slices. Place the panini on a baking sheet to take out to the grill.

Prepare enough coals for a medium-hot charcoal fire, or preheat your gas grill on medium-high for 10 minutes with the lid closed.

When the coals are ready or the gas grill is hot, place the panini on the grill and weigh them down with the bricks—1 brick should work for 2 panini. Grill for 3 minutes, making sure the bottom doesn't burn. Turn, place the bricks back on the panini, and grill for 3 minutes more. The cheese does not have to be completely melted; it'll still taste spectacular.

Slice each sandwich in half; serve immediately.

Tears on My Pillow

"DAD, PROMISE YOU WON'T SAY ANY-THING, but we rented this movie, *Revenge of the Nerds*, at my friend Gabriel's house the other night when I was sleeping over and Gabriel's dad was watching it with us, and at the end of the movie, when the nerds, like, get their revenge, he . . ."

"He what?"

"Gabriel's dad, he *cried*. He turned away so we couldn't see, but he was actually *crying* at the end of *Revenge of the Nerds*."

I was shocked. Not at the man's display of emotion, but at the daunting task I realized I now faced hiding my own tears from my son. *Bad News Bears*, for instance, does it to me every time, when that kid who hadn't caught a fly ball all season holds out his glove in right field (I used to play right field!) and miraculously the ball lands inside. Or the opening (and, for that matter, the middle and end) of *West Side Story*.

What can I say, I'm a guy who gets teary. I trace it back to my own father, who thoughtlessly gave me the Lou Gehrig bio *Pride of the Yankees* to read as a kid. From the moment the Iron Horse tells the skipper he isn't feeling too good that day to his "luckiest man in the world" speech at the stadium, I soaked every page with my tears. Now I'm stuck with them. The last scenes in *Gunga Din*, or when Babe won the sheep contest—forget about it. And *Of Mice and Men*—keep it away from me. I used to think I was doing something wrong, that I wasn't manly enough (me, who used to dunk over guys playing pickup basketball on West 4th Street). I won't try to justify or explain it to my sons. Instead, I've dug up my copy of *Pride of the Yankees*, which I'll soon be reading to them. Then we'll see who gets the last cry.

Panino Monstro

As long as you've got a grill, you might as well make a panino that you would be hard-pressed to find a skillet big enough to encompass. Cut this up and let everyone have a piece. Then make another one. **Serves 4 to 6**

Ingredients

1 focaccia, approximately 12 inches square, sliced in half horizontally

Olive oil, for brushing

One 2-ounce jar basil pesto

5 ounces hard Italian salami, thinly sliced

One 4-ounce jar roasted red peppers, drained and cut into thin strips

4 ounces fresh baby spinach leaves, washed and dried

1 small red onion, thinly sliced

4 ounces provolone cheese, thinly sliced

2 bricks wrapped in foil, or other suitable weight

→ **Brush** the outside of each focaccia slice with olive oil. Lightly brush the inside of each slice with pesto.

Arrange the salami slices on the bottom half of the focaccia. Arrange the roasted pepper strips, spinach, and red onion over the salami. Top with the slices of provolone. Place the top half of the focaccia over everything.

Prepare enough coals for a medium-hot charcoal fire, or preheat your gas grill on medium-high for 10 minutes with the lid closed.

When the coals are ready or the gas grill is hot, place the panino on the grill and weigh it down with the bricks. Grill for 3 minutes, making sure the bottom doesn't burn. Turn; you may need to use 2 spatulas to do this and possibly another set of hands. Place the bricks back on top, and grill for 3 minutes more. The cheese does not have to be completely melted.

Slice into 2, 4, or 8 panini, depending on who is eating it, and serve.

Leftover Chicken & Cheddar Quesadillas

You can prepare these with pretty much leftover anything—lamb, steak, pork. Don't tell anyone, but sometimes I buy a free-range rotisserie chicken and pull the meat off it for quesadillas. However you get there, the result is a family-friendly entrée that, once assembled and wrapped in foil, is ready in minutes. **Serves** 4

Ingredients

1 pound leftover cooked chicken, cut into about ½-inch pieces

4 ounces hot smoked sausage, finely chopped

1 cup jarred salsa

One 4-ounce can diced green chiles, drained

1 chipotle chile in adobo, coarsely chopped

1 tablespoon chili powder

1 teaspoon ground cumin

1 teaspoon salt

8 quesadilla-size flour tortillas

2 cups grated Cheddar cheese

→ **In** a large bowl, place the chicken pieces along with the sausage, ¼ cup of the salsa, the green chiles, chipotle, chili powder, cumin, and salt, and mix together until well combined.

To assemble the quesadillas, lay a tortilla in the center of a 16-inch-long piece of aluminum foil. Spread one-eighth of the cooled chicken mixture evenly over one side of the tortilla. Top with one-eighth of the cheese. Fold the tortilla over and wrap in the foil. Repeat with the remaining tortillas, filling, and cheese.

Pack the wrapped quesadillas flat in a container and refrigerate, unless grilling right away.

Prepare enough coals for a medium charcoal fire, or preheat your gas grill on medium for 10 minutes with the lid closed.

When the coals are ready or the gas grill is hot, lay the aluminum-wrapped quesadillas on the grate, and grill for 4 minutes. Turn and grill for 3 minutes more.

Remove the quesadillas from the foil and lay each one directly on the grate. Cook for about 1 minute more on each side, until they begin to get some grill marks.

Transfer to a platter and let them cool for a few minutes, so no one burns their mouth on the filling, and serve with the remaining salsa.

Note: *You can replace the chicken and/or sausage with equal amounts of leftover cooked steak, pork, hamburger, or fish.*

Pulled Pork Sandwiches

Pulled pork is one of the barbecue fundamentals. It feeds a crowd and it makes that fed crowd happy. It does require most of the afternoon to cook, so while it's cooking you could undertake one of those projects you've been diligently putting off, like instead of possibly getting ready to maybe begin thinking about the likelihood of potentially perhaps preparing to get started cleaning the garage, you could actually do it. Four hours later you will have the most flavorful, succulent meat you've ever tasted and the satisfaction of crossing something off the to-do list.

Serves 8 to 10

Ingredients

3 tablespoons sweet paprika

2 tablespoons chili powder

2 tablespoons ground cumin

2 tablespoons brown sugar

2 tablespoons kosher salt

1 tablespoon ground black pepper

1 tablespoon sugar

1 bone-in Boston butt or pork shoulder, 6 to 8 pounds

2 cups of hickory or other hardwood chips

3 cups Dad's All-Purpose Barbecue Sauce (page 180)

20 slices white bread

→ **In** a small bowl, mix together the paprika, chili powder, cumin, brown sugar, salt, pepper, and sugar until well combined.

Cut away any skin from the pork (you can ask the butcher to do this if you want, but it's not hard.) Rub the entire roast with the spices, wrap it in plastic, and refrigerate at least 12 hours and up to 24 hours.

Two hours before cooking, soak the wood chips in water to cover.

Prepare enough coals for a medium fire. While the coals are heating up, unwrap the pork and place it in an aluminum pan just big enough to hold it.

Lay a 12-inch, double-layer of aluminum foil on a work surface. Place half the wood chips in the center, then fold to make a neat package. Poke 6 holes in the top to release the smoke during cooking.

When the coals are hot, distribute them on opposite sides of the grill and open the bottom vents. Place one hickory chip package directly on one of the piles of coals and set the grill rack in place. Set the pork pan in the center of the rack and cover the grill, making sure the bottom grill vents and the cover vents are open. Smoke for 3 hours, adding a handful of coals every 40 minutes or so. Halfway through cooking, place the second wood chip package on the coals.

Twenty minutes before you finish smoking, preheat the oven to 325° F.

Remove the pan with the pork from the grill, cover it tightly with foil, and transfer it to the oven. Cook on the center rack for 2 hours.

Remove the pan from the oven and let it sit for 1 hour.

Unwrap the foil and transfer the pork to a cutting board. When cool enough to handle, separate the large pieces of meat from the bone and shred it with your fingers. Toss the shredded pork with 1 cup of barbecue sauce, adding more to taste, but not too much, as people will add more later when they make their sandwiches.

Grilled Veggie Muffuletta

Muffuletta has its origins somewhere in New Orleans, invented either by Signor Lupo Salvadore at the cozy family–run Italian market the Central Grocery or by a chef at the Napoleon House, a restaurant in the French Quarter, located on the ground floor of a house that was actually constructed for Napoleon, in the hope that he would spend his life in exile by the banks of the Mississippi. Napoleon never arrived, even though they built a widow's walk for him so he could look out over the water and contemplate his comeback. **Serves 4**

Ingredients

One 4-ounce jar roasted red peppers, drained and cut into 1-inch strips

One 4-ounce jar artichoke hearts, drained and cut into quarters

½ cup pitted kalamata olives

¼ cup raisins, plumped for 5 minutes in very hot water and drained

1 teaspoon balsamic vinegar

¼ cup fresh parsley

¾ cup extra virgin olive oil

1 eggplant, peeled and cut into ½-inch slices

1 large sweet onion, cut into ½-inch slices

1 portobello mushroom, about 4 inches across, stemmed and cut into ½-inch slices

Salt and freshly ground black pepper

1 large, round, flat loaf sourdough bread

6 Roma tomatoes, cut in half lengthwise and seeded, then cut into ½-inch dice

4 ounces fontina cheese, thinly sliced

→ **Place** the roasted peppers, artichoke hearts, olives, raisins, vinegar, and parsley in the bowl of a food processor, along with $\frac{1}{2}$ cup of the olive oil, and pulse just a few times, until everything is finely chopped but not smooth. You'll need to work in short pulses to achieve this. Transfer the olive mixture to a bowl and set aside, or cover and refrigerate for up to 48 hours.

Prepare enough coals for a hot charcoal fire, or preheat your gas grill on high for 10 minutes with the lid closed.

While the grill is heating, brush each side of the eggplant, onion, and mushroom slices with some of the remaining olive oil, and season to taste with salt and pepper.

When the coals are ready or the gas grill is hot, grill the vegetables over medium heat for 5 minutes, until they are golden brown. Turn and grill for 4 to 5 minutes more, until they are all cooked through. You may have to take some of the pieces off the grill earlier. Transfer to a platter.

Slice the bread in half horizontally and remove enough of the doughy inside from the top to make room for the fillings. Spread about $\frac{1}{4}$ cup of the olive salad and its oil on the bottom. Arrange the grilled veggies on top in even layers. Place the diced tomato over them, and then top with the cheese slices. Spread another $\frac{1}{4}$ cup of the olive salad over the top piece of bread and then place it in its proper spot on top of the sandwich.

Wrap the muffuletta in plastic wrap and put a weight on it for an hour or so before cutting into wedges and serving.

Grilled Pizza with Pepperoni & Mushrooms

Your grill always needs to be clean, but it needs to be especially clean to make pizza. The extra fussing is definitely worth it, for if you've never tasted a pizza fresh off the grill, you are in for an incredible treat. If it were easier to do, grilled pizza would be the standard. Not that it's wickedly complicated, just more so than sliding a pie into the oven. I advise preparing a double batch of pizza dough for your maiden pizza-grilling voyage. That way you can take a little batting practice to get your stroke and timing down. Grill a few pizzas with just sauce and cheese to get the hang of it and then, when you feel ready, knock one out of the park with all the toppings.

Makes four 12-inch pizzas

Ingredients

Pizza Dough (recipe follows)

Flour, for dusting

Spray cooking oil

2 tablespoons extra virgin olive oil

8 ounces white or cremini mushrooms, cut into ¼-inch slices

One 4-ounce jar roasted red peppers, drained well and cut into ¼-inch slices

1 tablespoon chopped fresh garlic

Salt and freshly ground black pepper

2 cups pizza sauce

8 ounces fresh mozzarella, grated

6 ounces pepperoni, thinly sliced

Cornmeal, for dusting

→ **Remove** the balls of pizza dough from the refrigerator. Clear a 2-foot-square area on the counter that you can use later for rolling out the dough.

Place a large, heavy bottomed skillet over medium-high heat. When the pan gets hot, add the olive oil, spreading it so it evenly coats the bottom of the pan. Add the mushrooms and cook them, stirring regularly, until they soften, about 7 minutes. Add the roasted peppers and garlic and cook for 1 minute more. Season with salt and pepper to taste and transfer to a medium bowl. Set aside or let cool, cover, and refrigerate for up to 24 hours.

Set the mushroom mixture, the pizza sauce, the grated cheese, and the pepperoni on a table near the grill. Prepare enough coals for a hot charcoal fire, or preheat your gas grill on high for 10 minutes with the lid closed.

While the grill is getting hot, generously dust a metal pizza tray or the back of a sheet pan with cornmeal. Also generously dust your clear counter area with flour.

Using a rolling pin and working from the center, roll out one ball of the dough into a 12-inch circle.

Transfer the dough to a pizza tray or the back of the sheet pan, making sure there is enough cornmeal to allow it to slide easily. Repeat with the other 3 pieces of dough, placing each one on a separate tray.

When the coals are ready or the gas grill is hot, bring one of the pizza trays to the grill and slide the dough onto the center of the grill grate. Grill for 2 to 3 minutes, or until golden brown. Turn over and immediately spoon a layer of sauce over the crust. Add some of the cheese, then some of the mushroom mixture, then some of the pepperoni.

Continue grilling for 2 to 3 more minutes, until the crust is cooked through (this may happen before the cheese melts completely— but that's okay).

Bring the pizza tray close to the grill and slide the pizza on to it. Transfer to a large cutting board. Have one of The Progeny use a pizza wheel to cut it into 6 pieces, and then transfer the slices to a large plate while you start working on the next pizza.

Pizza Dough

If you can find premade pizza dough you like in a local market or gourmet shop, by all means use it. If not, you'll find assembling this dough a quick and easy process once you get the hang of it. Remember to store any unused yeast in the refrigerator.

Makes four 12-inch pizzas crusts

Ingredients

4½ cups (20.25 ounces) unbleached high-gluten, bread, or all-purpose flour

1¾ teaspoons salt

2 teaspoons instant yeast

¼ cup extra virgin olive oil

1¾ cups water

Semolina flour or cornmeal, for dusting

Spray cooking oil

→ **Measure** the flour, salt, and yeast into a large bowl. With a large wooden spoon, stir in the oil and the water until all of the flour is absorbed. Continue stirring the dough vigorously into a smooth mass. If the dough is too wet and doesn't come off the sides of the bowl, sprinkle in some more flour just until the dough clears the sides.

Sprinkle flour on the counter and knead the dough for 5 to 7 minutes until it is springy, elastic, and slightly sticky. Prepare a sheet pan by lining it with baking parchment and misting the parchment with spray oil (or lightly oil the parchment). Using a serated knife, cut the dough into 4 equal pieces. Make sure your hands are dry, and then flour them. Lift each piece and gently round it into a ball. Transfer the dough balls to the sheet pan, mist the dough generously with spray oil, and slip the pan into a clean plastic bag.

Put the pan into the refrigerator overnight to rest the dough. It will keep there for up to 2 days.

Note: *If you want to save some of the dough for future baking, you can freeze it. Dip each dough ball to be frozen into a bowl that has a few tablespoons of oil in it, rolling the dough in the oil to coat it, and then put each ball into a separate resealable freezer bag. You can place the bags into the freezer for up to 3 months. Transfer them to the refrigerator the day before you plan to make pizza.*

Grilled Pizza with Shrimp & Feta

A great pizza combo: just exotic enough to be different, just familiar enough to be in the regular pizza rotation. This oregano, shrimp, and feta ensemble has a Greek feel to it, so you can grill it up while The Progeny are in the basement building their models of the Parthenon. (The columns were Doric; the carved women were called caryatids.) **Makes two 12-inch pizzas**

Ingredients

2 balls (half recipe) Pizza Dough (recipe on facing page)

Flour, for dusting

Spray cooking oil

One 15-ounce can diced tomatoes, drained

1 cup grated mozzarella cheese

½ cup crumbled feta cheese

2 cloves garlic, finely chopped

2 tablespoons chopped fresh basil

1 teaspoon dried oregano

Red pepper flakes (optional)

4 bamboo skewers

Cornmeal, for dusting

8 ounces large shrimp (21–25 size), peeled and deveined

¼ cup extra virgin olive oil

Salt and freshly ground black pepper

→ **Remove** the balls of pizza dough from the refrigerator. Clear a 2-foot-square area on the counter that you can use later for rolling out the dough.

Place the tomatoes, mozzarella, feta, garlic, basil, oregano, and optional red pepper flakes in their own separate small bowls, and arrange them near the grill.

One hour before grilling, soak the bamboo skewers in warm water.

Prepare enough coals for a medium-hot fire, or preheat your gas grill on medium-high for 10 minutes with the lid closed.

While the grill is getting hot, generously dust a metal pizza tray or the back of a sheet pan with cornmeal. Also generously dust your clear counter area with flour.

Using a rolling pin and working from the center, roll out one ball of the dough into a 12-inch circle.

Transfer the dough to a pizza tray or the back of the sheet pan, making sure there is enough cornmeal to allow it to slide easily.

Continued on next page

Grilled Pizza with Shrimp & Feta (continued)

When the coals are ready or the gas grill is hot, thread the skewers through the shrimp, then brush them with olive oil and season with salt and pepper. Grill the shrimp on the medium-high side of the grill until they are cooked through, about 2½ minutes per side. Transfer to a platter.

Brush the pizza dough with olive oil, season with salt, and grill, oiled side down, for about 2 minutes, or until golden brown. Turn over and immediately add half the tomatoes, mozzarella, feta, and shrimp, trying to distribute them as evenly as possible but sacrificing aesthetics for speed. Then add half the garlic, basil, oregano, and red pepper flakes, if using. Cover or close the grill and grill for 2 to 3 minutes, until the bottom crust is golden brown. (The feta may not be completely melted.)

Bring the pizza tray close to the grill and slide the pizza onto it. Transfer the pizza to a large cutting board and cut into slices with a pizza wheel. Serve immediately while you make the second pizza.

How to Order Off Any Wine List

PEOPLE WHO *think* they know about wine make a big deal of first burrowing their nose into the glass and breathing in deeply as they allow a dollop of wine to dribble into their mouth, where they allow it to wash around their tongue. They then make pronouncements about its *nose* and its *fruity notes* and its *finish*. But people who *really* know about wine just drink it, albeit slowly, and then say something like, "Hey, that's good" or "That's really good" or "That's really f***ing good."

In that cavalier spirit, here are two strategies for navigating through most any wine list that will make you look good in front of your kids.

Solution 1

If it's a restaurant that prides itself on its wine list, there should be a sommelier lurking around somewhere. Tell the waiter politely that you'd like to speak to him (or her). As he's on his way over, remind yourself that sommeliers have the same degree of contempt for wine *snobs* that they do for wine *idiots*.

When the sommelier arrives, say the following, sticking resolutely to the script:

"I'm looking for a _____ (red/white)."

Then point to any appropriately priced wine on the list and say, **"I'm thinking about something in this price range."**

Continue with either, **"I'm looking for a red with _____ (a bit of oak/a touch of fruit)"** or **"a white that _____ (is bone dry/is not bone dry)."**

The sommelier will now point to some wines. Let him identify three, then go with the first one he chooses, *unless*, and this is important, the name includes any of the following: the word "pond," flying animals that have no business flying or any similar kinds of oxymoronic constructs, references to any denizens of the underworld or popular culture, or puns of any kind.

Hand the sommelier the wine list, look him right in the eye, and say, **"Thank you for your help."**

Solution 2

If there's no sommelier, you will have to deal with the list on your own. The Progeny are watching, looking to see just how sophisticated their dad is.

Here's the secret to decoding a standard offering of 10 wines:

Wine 1. Never order this one. It's for losers. Guys who will call their mothers after the date. Who have a favorite brand of floss. Who order their breakfast specials with sliced tomato instead of home fries.

Wine 2. The restaurant's hoping you'll go here. They know you'll take a pass on the first wine (because everybody knows not to order it), so they set out this one as a trap. This vineyard used to be a miniature golf course. The vines grow through the remains of the windmill on what was once the seventh hole. Stay away.

Wine 3. The restaurant owner's putting his kid through college on this wine. It's for suckers only. Men who think they've beaten the system. Hah! This is the wine they've been trying to get rid of for years. At harvest time, it was a toss-up as to whether these grapes were better off as Hawaiian Punch.

Wine 5. Nooooo! This one is saved for men who still hope to run into their high school science teacher because they have so much to *tell* him, for guys who think, "What the hell. I don't know anything about wine; I'll pick the one in the middle. How could I go wrong?" Well, Junior, you just went

very wrong. This bottle is filled with the remnants from all the other bottles. That pop you heard when the cork came out? Well, Sonny Boy, the waiter did that with his mouth.

Wine 6. Okay, here's the first real wine. It's a serious bump up in price, so it must be better. And your impulse is to think, "Okay, I deserve it. Maybe I'm not ready for one of the *super* expensive wines, but this will be a first step." Wrong. It's the same as Wine 2, only with a different label. The vineyard does it for them special. Yes, it says "Reserve." But the only thing being reserved is a stateroom on a cruise the owner is taking this January with that fetching waitress leaning over the other table—a cruise being paid for solely by guys who order this very wine because they think they are "deserving." (Wish him bon voyage while you're at it.)

Wine 7. Up until this one, the wines have been in order of price. But Wine 7 is curiously cheaper than Wine 6. Is it a typo? An oversight? Or is it someone's devious way of suggesting that this wine, because it is surrounded by titans, is one itself? Don't be seduced. Wine 7 really is cheap, just with a classy label. They're hoping you'll let yourself be swayed, thinking you've found the one true bargain on the list.

Wines 8 and 9. These are good wines, but too expensive. Try to remember them the next time you are in a wine store.

Wine 10. Steer clear of No. 10. It's purposefully marked sky-high for dumb lugs trying impress someone.

Wine 4. This is the one. If you want you can take a moment to pretend you are considering some of the others, or—and this will really impress the kids—just run your finger along the list and stop at the fourth wine down. And when the waiter brings it to your table and opens it for you to taste, tell him he can just go ahead and pour.

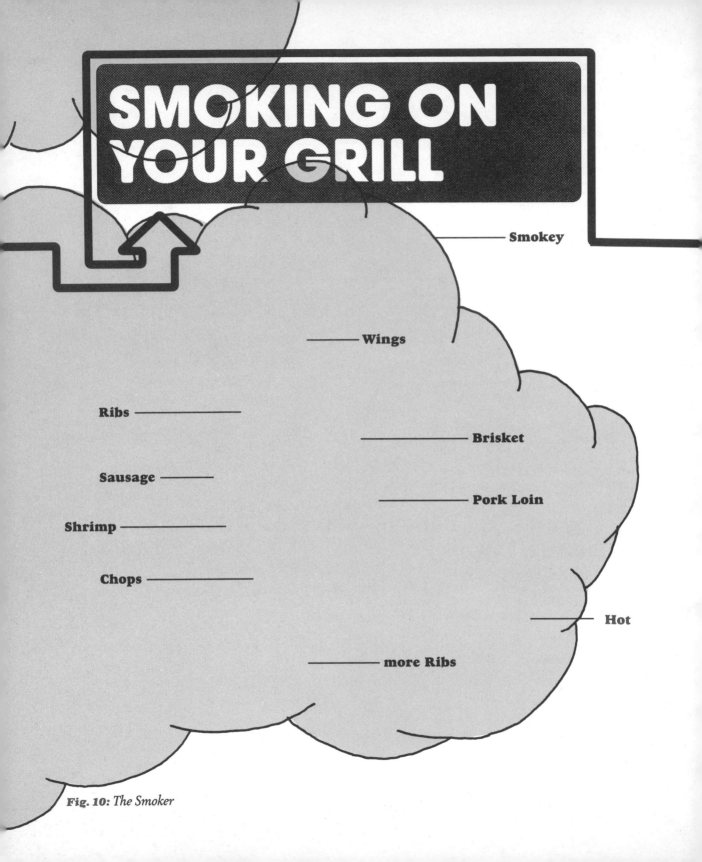

SMOKING ON YOUR GRILL

Smokey

Wings

Ribs

Brisket

Sausage

Pork Loin

Shrimp

Chops

Hot

more Ribs

Fig. 10: *The Smoker*

10

If you order at a real pit barbecue restaurant anywhere in this great land, I can guarantee you that no matter how good you think the place is— even if you made a pilgrimage to the legendary funky Southern juke joint out on a dirt road where the hickory smoke fills the entire county—the place that's been run by the same family for generations, the family that *invented* barbecue—that even *there*, someone in your party is going to reminisce about even *better* barbecue they had somewhere else. It's the nature of the beast.

Because the barbecue is *always* better at some other place.

I say this to encourage you. So you can aspire to barbecue perfection, knowing that achieving it is never quite possible.

The first thing you need to know about smoking is that it takes time. In a world where it seems speed is everything, you will be cooking at a pace closer to that of a Zamboni machine. But once you get used to the rhythm, you may find it a comforting antidote to the vicissitudes of this helter-skelter world.

Smoking is the process of cooking something over indirect heat for an extended period of time. While it is cooking, the mixture of spices you've carefully rubbed over the surface starts to permeate the food. Those flavors, coupled with the more subtle flavor of the smoke, give the meat, poultry, or fish its deep, distinctive taste.

The Grill

You will need to have a charcoal kettle grill or one of the many smokers on the market, all of which work on the same basic principle but with their own idiosyncratic process, so I will defer to their specific instructions. If you don't have either a smoker or a charcoal grill, you can do simple smoking on your gas grill, but it requires some finagling, meaning that you'll be much happier investing in an additional kettle-style grill or a separate smoker. You can try to discreetly use your neighbor's smoker while he's asleep, hoping the distinctive sweet, pungent smell of the smoking hardwood doesn't waft into his open window during the night. You can leave a few barbecued ribs in a wicker basket on his doorstep the next morning by way of a thank-you. Or not.

The Wood

The chips or chunks of hardwood can be hickory, cherry, oak, or some combination. The most important step is making sure to soak them for at least an hour before adding them to the fire, so they don't just flare up and burn out but instead "steam" a bit and slowly release their smoke.

The Dry Rub

Once you discover how much flavor you can impart to your meat with a dry rub, you will start looking for ways to dry-rub your cereal in the morning. Every barbecuing Dad should have his own basic rub recipe that can be enhanced as needed. You can prepare small jars of it in advance so it's always ready to go. You can put some in decorative spice jars and give them away as holiday gifts.

The simplest rubs are salt, pepper, sugar, and paprika. You can enhance that with garlic powder, onion powder, cumin, oregano, thyme, rosemary, or cayenne. The sugar helps draw the seasoning into the meat. Twelve hours is usually all pork, chicken, or beef need for the dry rub to have its maximum effect, though a whole pork shoulder for pulled pork might demand 24 hours of rub time. A salmon fillet needs just 2 hours—after that the rub will overwhelm the inherent flavor of the salmon.

The Brine

Brining chicken, salmon, and pork will make the meat more plump and juicy after you finish smoking it. The basic recipe is 1 cup kosher salt and ¼ cup sugar to 1 gallon of water. Make sure the salt and sugar are completely dissolved before adding the meat. You will need enough brine to completely submerge the meat without any part being out of the liquid. Brine the meat for about 1 hour per pound. Remove from the brine (don't reuse the brine), rinse to remove any excess salt, and cook.

Not Too Much Smoke

It is possible to oversmoke your food, in which case you will wind up with a slab of hickory ribs flavored with far more hickory than rib. There does not need to be a steady stream of smoke coming from the grill for the smokiness to be imparted to the food. Start with the amount of chips I suggest, then adjust according to your taste and the way your grill or smoker is working.

The Charcoal

Only a small pile of briquettes is necessary to generate the heat needed for proper smoking, which should be in the area of 200° to 225°F. The key is maintaining that steady heat, which requires adding a few coals to the pile every 30 minutes or so. The hinged flaps on the new Webers make this process a breeze.

The Drip Pan

Place a rectangular aluminum pan with an inch of water on the coal grate under the meat. This catches dripping fat and helps prevent flare-ups.

Kansas City-Style Beef Ribs

Kansas City is one of the capitals of smoked food, with a barbecue culture all its own. The classic Kansas City sauce is sort of a marriage of Southern and Texas flavors—it's got a touch of sweetness with a distinctive kick. They'll smoke just about anything in K.C. They especially like these beef ribs, which are big and meaty, like props in a caveman movie, only bigger. **Serves 4**

Ingredients

2 cups pineapple juice

¼ cup Worcestershire sauce

1 medium onion, thinly sliced

2 tablespoons extra virgin olive oil

¼ cup apple cider vinegar

3 tablespoons white sugar

1 teaspoon Dijon-style mustard

4 pounds beef ribs

2 tablespoons sweet paprika

1 tablespoon brown sugar

1 teaspoon garlic powder

1 teaspoon freshly ground black pepper

½ teaspoon salt

4 cups wood chips, preferably hickory or oak

1 cup favorite Kansas City-style barbecue sauce, plus more for serving

➜ **Combine** the pineapple juice, Worcestershire sauce, onion, olive oil, cider vinegar, white sugar, and mustard in a large bowl. Add the beef ribs and toss so they are coated on all sides. Cover and refrigerate for at least 4 hours and up to 24 hours.

Combine the paprika, brown sugar, garlic powder, black pepper, and salt in a small bowl and stir together.

At least 1 hour before grilling, soak the wood chips in water.

Remove the ribs from the marinade and pat them dry with paper towels. Sprinkle them with the spice mixture so it evenly coats the ribs, and let them sit at room temperature while you heat up the grill.

Prepare enough coals for a medium fire, or set your smoker to 200° to 220°F.

Just before grilling, drain the wood chips. Use 12-inch sheets of aluminum foil to make 4 packages of chips. Poke some holes in the tops of the packages to release the smoke during cooking.

When the coals are ready, arrange them on one side of the coal grate, in as compact a pile as possible. Place one of the wood chip packets on the hot coals. Set a 9-by-12-inch aluminum pan on the opposite side of the coal grate and add 1 inch of water to the pan. Place the ribs on the grill rack, away from the coals and over the pan, setting them as close together as possible without touching. Cover the grill, positioning the vent over the ribs.

Smoke the ribs for about 3 hours, or until tender. Add a few more coals and another packet of wood chips every hour.

Place a large sheet of foil on the work surface. Transfer the cooked ribs to the center of the foil. Pour the barbecue sauce over them so it evenly coats the ribs. Seal the ribs in the foil for 30 minutes to let the sauce infuse the meat.

Unwrap and serve with more sauce.

POP CULTURE
Grill Gifts for Dad

AROUND THE HOLIDAYS, your birthday, or Father's Day, you may want to leave this book around the house in a conspicuous place, casually open to this page, to ensure that you get exactly what you need.

A chip box: A sturdy metal container with holes in it to hold your soaked wood chips.

A fish spatula: Wide and thin, it allows you to get under the fillets and turn them with ease.

Metal skewers: Wood works well when soaked, but it's classier to have a set of skewers you can rely on in any circumstance.

A new grill brush: Because I just know your old one is worn out.

Smoked Brisket

Down in Houston they are very particular about their smoked brisket. It has to be almost black on the outside and perfectly succulent inside. It has to have an ineluctable presence of smoke, but not so much that it overwhelms the natural flavor of the meat. In short, it has to be perfect. This recipe comes close. It also gives Dad a chance to wield a hefty hunk o' beef, which, if done with confidence, should leave an impression on The Progeny that their Dad, even if he can't fix a broken light socket, can at least wield a hefty hunk o' beef. **Serves 6 to 8**

Ingredients

1 beef brisket (about 4 pounds), with a half-inch layer of fat on top if possible

2 tablespoons dark brown sugar

2 tablespoons chili powder

2 tablespoons paprika

2 tablespoons salt

1 tablespoon garlic powder

1 tablespoon onion powder

1 tablespoon ground black pepper

1 tablespoon cayenne pepper

2 teaspoons dry mustard

2 teaspoons ground cumin

2 cups mesquite wood chips

Dad's All-Purpose Barbecue Sauce (page 180), for serving

→ **Lay** a double-wide 2-foot length of plastic wrap on the counter and set the brisket in the center of it.

In a medium bowl, thoroughly combine the brown sugar, chili powder, paprika, salt, garlic powder, onion powder, black pepper, cayenne pepper, dry mustard, and cumin. Rub the mixture into both sides of the brisket and then wrap it tightly in the plastic wrap. Place on a baking sheet and let marinate in the refrigerator for at least 6 hours or overnight.

At least 1 hour before grilling, soak the wood chips in water. Remove the meat from the refrigerator and let it come to room temperature.

Prepare enough coals for a medium fire, or set your smoker to 200° to 220°F.

Just before grilling, drain the wood chips. Use 12-inch sheets of aluminum foil to make 4 packages of chips. Poke some holes in the tops of the packages to release the smoke during cooking.

When the coals are ready, arrange them in a small pile on one side of the coal grate. Place a drip pan with ½ inch of water on the other side of the coal grate. Place one package of wood chips on the hot coals. Arrange the unwrapped brisket on the grill rack directly over the drip pan, and cover the grill.

Smoke the brisket for about 4½ hours, until it reaches an internal temperature of 180°F. Add a few more coals and another packet of wood chips every hour to maintain an even temperature.

Preheat the oven to 225°F.

When the meat reaches the desired temperature, remove it from the grill and wrap it in a double layer of foil. Place it on a sheet pan and set it on the middle rack of the oven for another hour.

Remove the brisket from the oven and unwrap the foil. Let it rest for 20 minutes before cutting it across the grain into ½-inch slices. Serve with the barbecue sauce.

Smoked Sausage, Pepper & Grilled Onion Sandwiches

Forget everything you've heard about nutrition, about healthful eating, about portions and fat, and, for one meal anyway, indulge in this big, succulent, wonderful, and inspiringly corpulent sandwich. Grill these up to celebrate an appropriately sizable accomplishment: a science award, winning a wrestling match, one of The Progeny has finally cleaned up their room. You won't regret it. **Makes 8 sandwiches**

Ingredients

¾ **cup wood chips**

8 **sweet or hot Italian sausages**

2 **tablespoons extra virgin olive oil**

2 **red bell peppers, stemmed, seeded, and cut into ½-inch slices**

1 **large onion, cut in half and then lengthwise into ¼-inch slices**

4 **cloves garlic, finely chopped**

8 **generous-sized rolls**

→ **At** least 1 hour before grilling, soak the wood chips in water.

Prepare enough coals for a medium fire, or set your smoker to 200° to 220°F.

Just before grilling, drain the wood chips. Use 12-inch sheets of aluminum foil to make 2 packages of chips. Poke some holes in the tops of the packages to release the smoke during cooking.

When the coals are ready, arrange them in a small pile on one side of the coal grate. Place a drip pan with ½ inch of water on the other side of the coal grate. Place one package of the wood chips on the hot coals. Arrange the sausages on the grill rack directly over the drip pan, and cover the grill.

Smoke the sausages for about 45 minutes, until they are a deep brown and cooked through. Halfway through cooking, add the second package of chips.

While the sausages are smoking, place a large, heavy-bottomed skillet over medium heat. When the pan gets hot, add the oil, spreading it so it evenly coats the bottom of the pan. Add the peppers and onions and cook, stirring regularly, until they soften, about 10 minutes. Add the garlic and cook for 1 minute more. Set aside.

When the sausages are done, transfer each to a roll and top with some of the onions, peppers, and garlic. Serve immediately.

Smoked Pork Chops

Slowly cooking pork chops is like putting training wheels on The Progeny's first two-wheeler—it gives you so much more margin for error. The result will be pork chops that are juicy and full of flavor. **Serves 4**

Ingredients

¼ cup plus 2 tablespoons brown sugar

1 cup, plus 1 teaspoon kosher salt

1 cup boiling water

1 gallon cold water

4 pork loin chops, 1½ inches thick

1½ cups hickory wood chips

1 teaspoon paprika

1 teaspoon caraway seeds

½ teaspoon ground allspice

½ teaspoon freshly ground black pepper

1 tablespoon vegetable oil

1 tablespoon apple cider vinegar

1 pound sauerkraut, for serving

Brown mustard, for serving

→ **At** least 6 hours before grilling, stir ¼ cup of the brown sugar and 1 cup of the salt into the boiling water until they are completely dissolved. Place the 1 gallon of cold water into a pasta pot and add the brown sugar solution. Submerge the pork chops in the brine and refrigerate for at least 4 hours and up to 8 hours.

One hour before grilling, soak the wood chips in enough water to cover.

In a small bowl, mix together the remaining 2 tablespoons brown sugar, the paprika, salt, caraway seeds, allspice, and black pepper. Stir in the oil and vinegar.

Remove the chops from the brine and pat dry with paper towels. Rub both sides of the chops with the spice mixture. Let the chops sit at room temperature while you ready the grill.

Prepare enough coals for a medium fire, or set your smoker to 200° to 220°F.

Just before grilling, drain the wood chips. Use 12-inch sheets of aluminum foil to make 2 packages of chips. Poke some holes in the tops of the packages to release the smoke during cooking.

When the coals are ready, arrange them on one side of the grill, in as compact a pile as possible. Place one of the wood chip packets on the hot coals. Set a 9-by-12-inch aluminum pan on the opposite side of the coal grate and add 1 inch of water to the pan. Place the pork chops on the grill rack, opposite the coals and above the pan, setting them as close together as possible without touching. Cover the grill, positioning the vent over the chops. Smoke the chops for about 1¾ hours, or until tender. Halfway through, add a few more coals and the second packet of chips.

Serve with the sauerkraut and brown mustard.

Bacon-Wrapped Smoked Loin of Pork

This pork is intense. The Progeny will definitely be impressed when you take it off the grill, as it's the kind of dish that they would expect to see only in a restaurant. The bacon gives it a vibrant crust (you should say that when first they taste it—"Isn't that a vibrant crust, kids?") that is balanced by the sweetness of the maple syrup. **Serves 6**

Ingredients

¼ cup firmly packed brown sugar

1 cup kosher salt

1 cup boiling water

1 gallon cold water

1 center-cut boneless pork loin
(about 4 pounds)

1½ cups wood chips

12 slices bacon

⅓ cup Dijon-style mustard

Freshly ground black pepper

1 cup pure maple syrup

→ **At** least 6 hours before grilling, stir the brown sugar and salt into the boiling water until it is completely dissolved. Place the 1 gallon of cold water into a pasta pot and add the brown sugar solution. Submerge the pork loin in the brine and refrigerate for at least 4 hours and up to 8 hours.

One hour before grilling, soak the wood chips in enough water to cover.

When you are ready to smoke it, remove the loin from the brine and pat it dry with paper towels. Arrange the bacon over the pork, and wrap the entire loin as tightly as possible, overlapping when necessary so you have no loose ends. Spread the mustard over the bacon. Season with lots of black pepper.

Prepare enough coals for a medium charcoal fire, or set your smoker to 200° to 220°F. While the coals are heating up, drain the wood chips. Use 12-inch sheets of aluminum foil to make

3 packages of chips. Poke holes in the tops of the packages to release the smoke during cooking.

Arrange the hot coals on one side of the grill, in as compact a pile as possible. Place one of the wood chip packets on the hot coals. Place a 9-by-12-inch aluminum pan on the opposite side of the coal grate. Add 1 inch of water to the pan. Place the loin on the grill rack, opposite the coals and above the pan. Cover the grill, positioning the vent over the loin.

Add more coals and another packet of chips every 40 minutes until the chips run out. After 1 hour, baste the loin with some of the maple syrup and rotate so the opposite side faces the heat. Smoke the loin for about 2½ hours, until the internal temperature of the meat reaches 145°F.

After taking the loin off the grill, wrap it tightly in foil and let it rest for 30 minutes before slicing and serving.

Smoked Baby-Back Ribs

The pressure is on Dad when he sets out to make these. Smoked baby-back ribs are the touchstone by which one's smoking skills are judged. However, just the idea that someone would *try* to make barbecued ribs is going to generate a lot of goodwill.
Serves 4

Ingredients

¼ cup paprika

3 tablespoons brown sugar

2 tablespoons salt

1 teaspoon garlic powder

1 teaspoon caraway seeds

½ teaspoon ground cumin

2 racks baby-back ribs

2 cups hickory or other hardwood chips, or 6 to 8 hickory or other hardwood chunks

2 cups Dad's All-Purpose Barbecue Sauce (page 180)

→ **In** a small bowl mix the paprika, brown sugar, salt, garlic powder, caraway seeds, and cumin together and rub them into both sides of the ribs. Let the ribs sit for 2 hours at room temperature, though it's best to wrap them in plastic and refrigerate for up to 24 hours.

One hour before grilling, soak the wood chips in enough water to cover.

Prepare enough coals for a medium charcoal fire, or set your smoker to 200° to 220°F. Just before grilling, drain the wood chips. Use 12-inch sheets of aluminum foil to make 3 neatly sealed packages of wood chips. Poke some holes in the tops of the packages to release the smoke during cooking.

Arrange the hot coals on one side of the coal grate, in as compact a pile as possible. Place one of the wood chip packets on the hot coals. Place a 9-by-12-inch aluminum pan on the opposite side of the coal grate. Add 1 inch of water to the pan. Place the ribs on the grill rack above the drip pan. Cover the grill, positioning the vent over the ribs.

Smoke the ribs for about 2 hours and 15 minutes, adding more coals and another packet of chips every 30 minutes until they are used up. After 1 hour, rearrange the ribs so the rack closer to the coals is on the outside edge.

Remove the ribs from the grill, wrap each rack individually in foil, and let them rest for 30 minutes. Transfer the racks to a cutting board and cut into individual ribs. Serve with the barbecue sauce.

Smoked Wings Buffalo-Style

You've had barbecued wings, but you may never have had *smoked* wings. Well, let me assure you—these wings take flight. They are not included in the appetizer section because it's very hard to consume only an appetizer's worth. An industrious dad might prep a batch of these and slip them on the grill or into the smoker while he's smoking something else. (Just thought I'd mention that.) You can then finish them in the sauce when the moment is right. **Serves 6 as an appetizer**

Ingredients

2 teaspoons chili powder

2 teaspoons paprika

1 teaspoon garlic powder

1 teaspoon salt

1 teaspoon freshly ground black pepper

1 teaspoon caraway seeds

1 teaspoon celery seeds

24 chicken wings

2 tablespoons extra virgin olive oil

1½ cups wood chips

1 cup honey

½ cup hot barbecue sauce, or more to taste (use your favorite, the hottest sauce you can stand)

→ **In** a small bowl, combine the chili powder, paprika, garlic powder, salt, black pepper, caraway seeds, and celery seeds and mix together.

Trim off the small portion from each wing and discard. Cut the remaining wing portions in half at the joint. Place the wings in a large bowl and add the spice mixture. Toss so the wings are evenly coated. Add the olive oil and toss again. Cover the bowl or transfer the coated wings to a resealable freezer bag and refrigerate for 1 hour or up to 4 hours.

One hour before grilling, soak the wood chips in enough water to cover.

Prepare enough coals for a medium charcoal fire, or set your smoker to 200° to 220°F. While the coals are heating up, drain the wood chips. Use 12-inch sheets of aluminum foil to make 2 packages of chips. Poke some holes in the tops of the packages to release the smoke during cooking.

Arrange the hot coals on one side of the grill, in as compact a pile as possible. Place one of the wood chip packets on the hot coals. Place a 9-by-12-inch aluminum pan on the opposite side of the coal grate. Add 1 inch of water to the pan.

Arrange the wings on the grill rack, opposite the coals and over the pan, setting them as close together as possible without touching. Cover the grill, positioning the vent over the wings.

Smoke the wings for about 25 minutes. Add a few more coals and the other packet of chips. Turn the wings and smoke for another 20 to 25 minutes.

While the wings are smoking, mix the honey and barbecue sauce together in a small sauce-pan and heat over medium heat until warmed through.

Remove the wings from the grill and transfer to a disposable foil pan. Pour the warm sauce over the wings and toss to coat evenly. Place the pan on the hot side of the grill and cook for another 15 minutes or so, until the glaze is finished the way you like.

Dad's All-Purpose Barbecue Sauce

Why make your own barbecue sauce when there are so many bottled sauces to choose from? Good question. Maybe you've found one you like—the ideal balance of sweetness and bite, with maybe just a touch of heat. If so, I say, "Lucky you." One less thing for a busy dad to worry about. Maybe this sauce will be your second favorite.

Makes 3 cups

Ingredients

1 tablespoon extra virgin olive oil

1 medium onion, finely chopped

5 cloves garlic, finely chopped

1½ cups ketchup

½ cup tomato paste

¾ cup fresh orange juice

¼ cup water

¼ cup fresh lemon juice

2 tablespoons red wine vinegar

2 tablespoons tomato paste

2 tablespoons honey

2 tablespoons brown sugar

2 tablespoons molasses

2 tablespoons Worcestershire sauce

2 tablespoons mustard

1 tablespoon chili powder

1 teaspoon liquid smoke

1 teaspoon ground cumin

1 teaspoon Tabasco or other hot sauce

Pinch ground cinnamon

Pinch ground cloves

→ **Place** a large heavy-bottomed saucepan over medium heat. Add the olive oil, and when it's hot, cook the onions, stirring frequently, until they soften, about 5 minutes. Add the garlic and cook for 1 minute longer.

Add all the remaining ingredients to the pan and bring to a boil. Immediately reduce the heat to low and simmer for 5 minutes, stirring frequently.

Let cool and refrigerate for up to 1 week.

Smoked Shrimp with Jalapeño Mayo

You need big shrimp for this, so they can stay on the grill long enough to pick up the flavor of the smoke. **Serves 4**

Ingredients

½ **cup wood chips**

1½ **pounds extra-large shrimp (16–20 size), shells left on**

½ **cup extra virgin olive oil**

¼ **cup fresh lime juice**

¼ **cup finely chopped garlic**

➜ **At** least 1 hour before grilling, soak the wood chips in water.

Prepare enough coals for a medium charcoal fire, or set your smoker to 200° to 220°F. Just before cooking, in a large bowl toss the shrimp in the olive oil, lime juice, garlic, black pepper, cayenne, paprika, onion powder, and salt so they are all fully coated.

Drain the wood chips and assemble them into an aluminum foil packet. Pierce the top of the packet in several places to let the smoke out.

Arrange the coals as far to one side of the coal grate as possible. Place the packet of wood chips on the hot coals. Set the grill rack in place and arrange the shrimp on the side away from the coals.

Cover the grill and smoke the shrimp for about 35 minutes, or until cooked through.

Remove from the grill and serve with a hearty portion of the Jalapeño Mayo on the side.

1 **tablespoon freshly ground black pepper**

1 **teaspoon cayenne pepper**

1 **teaspoon sweet paprika**

1 **tablespoon onion powder**

½ **teaspoon salt**

Jalapeño Mayo (recipe follows)

Jalapeño Mayo

You can't go wrong with this quick and easy sauce that adds a refreshing and exuberant accompaniment to the shrimp. **Makes about 1¾ cups**

Ingredients

¾ **cup mayonnaise**

½ **cup sour cream**

¼ **cup finely chopped scallions, green parts only**

One 4-ounce can chopped jalapeño chiles

2 **tablespoons fresh lime juice**

Salt and freshly ground black pepper

➜ **Blend** all the ingredients together in a small bowl, adding salt and pepper to taste. Refrigerate until needed or up to 48 hours.

10 SUPER-FAST, FOOLPROOF GRILLING RECIPES

The secret ingredient: soupçon of steak sauce

Medium-rare roast beef

One soft roll

Fig. 11: *Savory Roast Beef Sandwiches*

11

Moms have been reaping the benefits of generations of cookbooks and magazine articles designed to help them whip up a meal. Countless recipes have been created so mom can throw together tasty instant dinners, ten-minute entrees, fast and foolproof meals. Mom has had an arsenal of ways to expediently feed the family.

Now it's Dad's turn. These quick and easy recipes are just for you. Don't even let mom see them.

Some feature bottled sauces or other time-saving tactics. Don't fret. Even though I know you are, by now, totally devoted to making everything from scratch, part of assuming regular cooking duties (as opposed to the once-a-year-I'll-make-dinner-and-mess-up-the-kitchen-so-badly-I'll-never-be-asked-to-cook-again approach) is that you get cut some slack regarding your culinary altruism.

If you work fast and don't put on SportsCenter while you're cooking, you should be able to prep these recipes in the time it takes for the charcoals to heat up. And if the local branch of the Junior League calls up and asks you for a recipe for their new Time Saving Cookbook, I grant you permission to give them one of these.

Chicken Breasts with Sun-Dried Tomato Pesto

Lurking somewhere in the supermarket, hidden on the shelves among the pasta sauces and tomato paste, you should see a small jar of deep red pesto made from sun-dried tomatoes. It has a wonderfully intense flavor that ennobles chicken breasts, with little more effort than it takes to apply toothpaste to your brush. **Serves 4**

Ingredients

One 4-ounce jar sun-dried tomato pesto

4 skinless, boneless chicken breast halves, pounded flat

→ **Prepare** enough coals for a hot charcoal fire, or preheat your gas grill on high for 10 minutes with the lid closed.

While the grill is getting hot, spread a thin layer of the sun-dried tomato pesto on both sides of each chicken breast.

When the coals are ready or the gas grill is hot, grill the chicken breasts for 3 minutes, until just golden brown. Turn and grill for about 3 minutes more, until they are just cooked through.

Transfer to a platter and serve.

Boneless Chicken Thighs Drenched with BBQ Sauce

This is your basic barbecued chicken. There are no bones, so the thighs cook relatively quickly. You just need to mop them generously with sauce toward the end of their stint on the grill, and they will reward you with a surprising amount of classic barbecue flavor. **Serves 4**

Ingredients

1 tablespoon chili powder

1 teaspoon garlic powder

½ teaspoon salt

12 skinless, boneless chicken thighs

2 tablespoons vegetable oil

2 cups jarred barbecue sauce

→ **In** a small bowl, combine the chili powder, garlic powder, and salt. Place the chicken thighs in a large bowl and add the spice mixture. Pour the oil over them and toss the thighs so they are all evenly coated.

Prepare enough coals for a medium-hot charcoal fire, or preheat your gas grill on medium-high for 10 minutes with the lid closed.

When the coals are ready or the gas grill is hot, grill the chicken thighs for 4 minutes, until just golden brown. Turn and grill for 3 to 4 minutes more, until they are cooked through. Mop the thighs on both sides several times with barbecue sauce during the last 2 minutes of cooking. Transfer to a platter and serve immediately.

Herbed Lemon Pork Chops

Though Dad can make these chops in his sleep, they have no shortage of flavor.
Serves 4

Ingredients

½ **cup fresh lemon juice**

½ **cup bottled Italian dressing**

1 **teaspoon Dijon-style mustard**

4 **boneless pork loin chops
(6 ounces each)**

➔ **In** a small bowl, combine the lemon juice, dressing, and mustard. Place the pork chops in a large bowl and pour two-thirds of the marinade over it, reserving the rest. Let them sit at room temperature while you light the fire.

Prepare enough coals for a medium-hot charcoal fire, or preheat your gas grill on medium-high for 10 minutes with the lid closed. When the coals are ready or the gas grill is hot, grill the pork chops for 6 minutes. Turn and grill for 5 to 6 minutes more, until they are just cooked through. Mop with the reserved marinade every few minutes during grilling.

Transfer to a platter and serve immediately.

Apricot-Glazed Ham Steak

This is a practically instant dinner. There are some quality ham steaks available in the supermarket, but to really make this recipe shine, see if you can find a shop that carries ham from a small, artisanal smokehouse. It will have a depth of flavor and texture that will be immediately apparent. **Serves 4**

Ingredients

½ **cup apricot preserves**

1 **tablespoon fresh lime juice**

2 **teaspoons coarse-grained mustard**

½ **teaspoon ground ginger**

Pinch freshly ground nutmeg

2 **boneless ham steaks, about
½ inch thick (12 to 14 ounces)**

➔ **In** a small saucepan, mix together the apricot preserves, lime juice, mustard, ginger, and nutmeg.

Prepare enough coals for a medium-hot charcoal fire, or preheat your gas grill on medium-high for 10 minutes with the lid closed.

When the coals are ready or the gas grill is hot, place the saucepan with the apricot glaze in a corner of the grill. Grill the ham steak for 6 minutes, turning once, until it is heated through. Brush the top with the glaze, turn, and grill for 1 minute. Repeat with the other side.

Transfer the ham steak to a platter, brush both sides once more with the glaze, and serve.

Citrus Shrimp

If you really want to speed things up, you can buy the shrimp already peeled and deveined. **Serves** 4

Ingredients

8 **bamboo skewers**

1 **grapefruit, peeled and cut into 1-inch pieces**

1 **small red onion, finely chopped**

¼ **cup fresh lime juice**

¼ **cup fresh orange juice**

½ **cup coarsely chopped fresh cilantro**

1 **tablespoon finely chopped jalapeño chile**

1 **teaspoon salt**

1½ **pounds extra-large shrimp (21–26 size), peeled and deveined**

Spray cooking oil

→ **One** hour before grilling, soak the bamboo skewers in warm water.

In a large bowl, combine the grapefruit sections, onion, lime juice, orange juice, cilantro, jalapeño, and salt. Set aside.

Prepare enough coals for a hot charcoal fire, or preheat your gas grill on high for 10 minutes with the lid closed.

While the coals are heating up, thread the shrimp onto the skewers, making sure not to crowd them.

When the coals are ready or the gas grill is hot, liberally spray the kabobs on all sides with cooking oil and grill them for 6 minutes, turning once, until they are just cooked through.

De-skewer the shrimp into the bowl with the citrus marinade and toss them gently so they are all coated. Serve immediately.

Grilled Lemon Rosemary Salmon in Foil

You can assemble these in the morning and leave them in the refrigerator, so once you get home from that hard day at the ~~links~~ office, you'll only need to heat up the grill.

Serves 4

Ingredients

Spray cooking oil

4 salmon fillets (6 ounces each)

Salt and freshly ground black pepper

1 lemon, thinly sliced

4 sprigs rosemary

4 tablespoons (½ stick) butter, cut into small pieces

4 fresh or dried sage leaves, coarsely chopped

→ **Cut** four 16-inch lengths of foil and lay them on the work surface. Spray with cooking oil.

Place a salmon fillet in the center of each piece of foil and season to taste with salt and pepper. Lay 3 lemon slices on each fillet. Lay 1 sprig of rosemary over the lemon. Dot with the butter and sprinkle with the chopped sage.

Bring the long ends of the foil together and fold them tightly several times. Then fold up the sides to make a neat, sealed packet.

Prepare enough coals for a hot charcoal fire, or preheat your gas grill on high for 10 minutes with the lid closed.

When the coals are ready or the gas grill is hot, lay the fish packets on the grill and cook for 14 minutes.

Open the packets carefully to avoid the escaping steam, and serve.

Savory Roast Beef Sandwiches

There are all kinds of ways to gussy up a roast beef sandwich: Russian dressing, coleslaw, cranberry sauce…I like this one because it's just roast beef and bread and a soupçon (I was hoping to get that word in somehow) of steak sauce.

Makes 4 sandwiches

Ingredients

⅓ **cup steak sauce, plus more for serving**

¼ **cup bottled Italian dressing**

2 **pounds top round steak,
  cut 1½ inches thick**

4 **soft rolls, or 8 slices white bread**

→ **In** a small bowl, combine the steak sauce and Italian dressing. Coat the steak with half the marinade and set aside while you light the grill.

Prepare enough coals for a two-tiered fire, hot on one side, medium on the other, or preheat your gas grill on high on one side and medium on the other for 10 minutes with the lid closed.

Grill the steak on the hot side of the grill for 4 minutes, until it is nicely browned. Turn and cook for 4 minutes more.

Brush the steak liberally with some of the remaining marinade, turn, and transfer to the medium side of the grill. Cook for 4 more minutes, then brush again with the marinade. Turn and cook for 3 to 4 minutes more, until it reaches 135°F on a meat thermometer for medium-rare. Turn the beef several times to cook it evenly, and brush liberally with the reserved marinade during the last few minutes.

Let the meat rest for 10 minutes, then cut it across the grain into the thinnest slices you can. Place a few slices of meat on the bottom half of each split roll or on 4 slices of bread. Pour any drippings into the bowl with the remaining marinade, and spread some on the top half of the roll or the top slice of bread. Serve the sandwiches with steak sauce.

Grilled Veal Chops with Savory Butter

If you make these veal chops for The Progeny, you should clue them in that they are being served something really special. Save them for a birthday, perhaps. Maybe yours. The compound butter takes a few minutes to prepare, but it lasts in the refrigerator for a while and becomes an instant sauce for many a grilled meat or fish. **Serves 4**

Ingredients

4 tablespoons (½ stick) butter, softened

4 cloves garlic, finely chopped

2 tablespoons finely chopped fresh rosemary

1 tablespoon finely chopped fresh thyme

4 loin or rib veal chops, each about 1 inch thick (8 to 10 ounces each)

2 tablespoons extra virgin olive oil

Salt and freshly ground black pepper

→ **Place** the softened butter in a medium bowl. Add the garlic, rosemary, and thyme and stir to combine. Place the butter mixture on a 12-inch piece of plastic wrap and roll into a log about 1 inch thick. Refrigerate until ready to use, or up to 1 month.

Brush both sides of the veal chops with the olive oil, and season to taste with salt and pepper.

Prepare enough coals for a medium-hot charcoal fire, or preheat your gas grill on medium-high for 10 minutes with the lid closed.

When the coals are ready or the gas grill is hot, cook the chops for 6 minutes. Turn and cook for 5 to 6 minutes more, until they are medium-rare.

Transfer the chops to a platter. Top each one with several pats of the butter, and let them rest for 5 minutes before serving.

Grilled Scallops with Sweet Chili Sauce

I happen to love scallops on the grill. You need to get the biggest ones you can find, however, and get the grill very hot. That way the scallops will form a nice crust on the outside. **Serves** 4

Ingredients

8 **bamboo skewers**

2 **tablespoons sesame oil**

2 **tablespoons vegetable oil**

1 **cup jarred sweet chili sauce**

16 **large sea scallops, crescent-shaped membrane removed**

12 **large shiitake mushrooms, stems removed**

6 **ounces mesclun salad**

→ **One** hour before grilling, soak the bamboo skewers in warm water.

Combine the sesame oil, vegetable oil, and 2 tablespoons of the chili sauce in a medium bowl. Add the scallops and shiitake mushrooms and toss so they are uniformly covered.

Prepare enough coals for a hot charcoal fire, or preheat your gas grill on high for 10 minutes with the lid closed.

While the coals are heating up, thread 4 scallops onto each of 4 skewers, making sure not to crowd them. On the remaining 4 skewers, thread the mushrooms across the circumference, as one would secure a hat with a hat pin.

When the coals are ready or the gas grill is hot, grill the scallop and mushroom skewers for 2 minutes, turn, and grill for 2 minutes more, until the scallops are just cooked through.

Transfer the skewers to a serving platter and serve with a bowl of the remaining sweet chili sauce, accompanied by the salad greens.

Steak Tacos

Even on a Sunday afternoon, when I have lots of time to cook, The Progeny clamor for these tacos. They may be basic, but they are also perfect. Try to find a really good jar of chili sauce or taco sauce to accompany them. **Serves** 4

Ingredients

1½ **pounds skirt steak**

2 **tablespoons chili powder**

2 **tablespoons garlic powder**

Salt and freshly ground black pepper

12 **corn tortillas**

One **12-ounce jar chipotle salsa**

4 **ounces Monterey Jack cheese, grated**

3 **limes, quartered into wedges**

→ **Season** both sides of the skirt steaks with chili powder, garlic powder, and salt and pepper to taste. Set aside while you light the grill.

Wrap the tortillas in aluminum foil in 3 packages of 4 tortillas each and set aside. Preheat the oven to 225°F.

Prepare enough coals for a hot charcoal fire, or preheat your gas grill on high for 10 minutes with the lid closed. Put the tortilla packages in the warm oven.

When the coals are ready or the gas grill is hot, grill the skirt steaks for 4 minutes, until they are nicely browned. Turn and grill for 4 to 5 minutes more, until they are medium.

Transfer the steaks to a cutting board and cut them into ¾-inch-thick slices. Transfer the sliced meat to a platter and set it on a serving table with the warm tortillas, salsa, grated cheese, and lime wedges; let everyone assemble their own tacos.

SIDES & DESSERTS

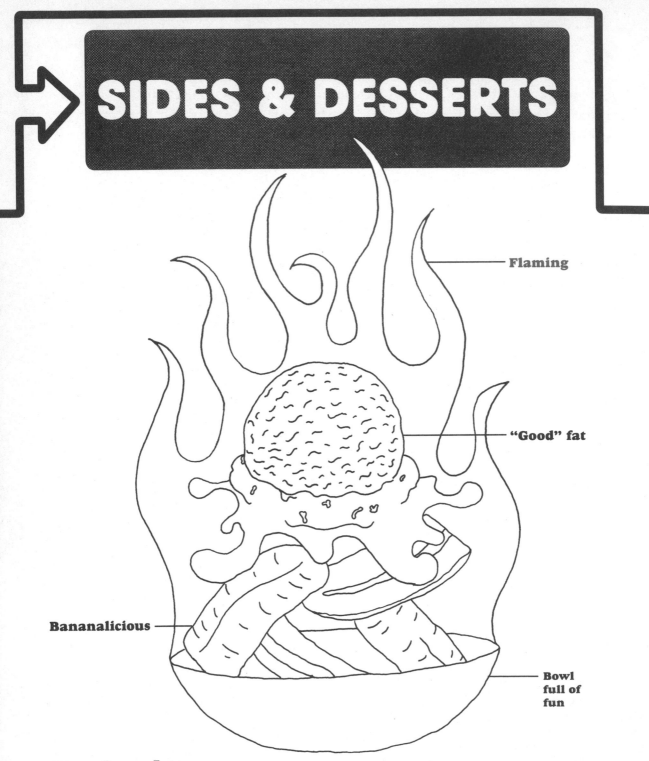

Flaming

"Good" fat

Bananalicious

Bowl full of fun

Fig. 12: *Bananas Foster*

12

Argh. Sides.
Wouldn't it be swell if you could accompany a grilled porterhouse steak with another grilled porterhouse steak?

Then you wouldn't have to be in the kitchen and the backyard at the same time. Maybe on your birthday you could get away with it. But for most meals, people expect a starch and a vegetable of some kind to accompany what comes off the barbecue.

Cowards.

Many dads are completely at ease with whatever is on their grill, but as soon as they have to start orchestrating one or two side dishes in concert with, say, the burgers or grilled fish, they start to get anxious. I've tried to eradicate that anxiety by including several sides that you can fit on the grill next to the main course. Others can be prepared in advance and then either reheated just before serving or served at room temperature.

Managing the sides can eventually become the responsibility of The Progeny. Eventually they will be able to cater their own weddings.

Like the other recipes in *Dad's Awesome Grill Book*, these desserts have been Dad-proofed. They're simple, straightforward, and if you actually do follow the directions (there's no "winging it" with baking, like you did when you tried to assemble that crib) you will produce the proper delicious results. Master the supple art of Double Chocolate Brownies and your cooking skills will be in demand even when there's too much snow to get to the grill.

White Bean, Smoked Sausage & Artichoke Salad

This a hearty salad that you might want to put on a buffet when you are serving a lighter main course, such as grilled striped bass fillets. I use a smoked chicken chorizo-style sausage, as it adds a bit of spice to the salad. **Serves 4**

Ingredients

¼ cup extra virgin olive oil

2 tablespoons sherry vinegar

1 teaspoon Dijon-style mustard

Salt and freshly ground black pepper

4 bamboo skewers

12 ounces chicken chorizo sausage, cut into ½-inch rounds

1 red bell pepper, stemmed, seeded, and cut into 1-inch pieces

2 small zucchini, about 1 inch thick, cut into ½-inch rounds

Spray cooking oil

4 leaves Boston lettuce

One 6-ounce jar artichoke hearts, drained and quartered

One 12-ounce can white beans, drained

½ cup chopped fresh parsley

½ cup chopped fresh basil

→ **Combine** the olive oil, vinegar, mustard, and salt and pepper to taste and whisk together until well combined. Set aside or cover and refrigerate for up to 1 week.

One hour before grilling, soak the bamboo skewers in warm water.

Prepare enough coals for a hot charcoal fire, or preheat your gas grill on high for 10 minutes with the lid closed.

While the coals are heating up, thread the sausage, red pepper, and zucchini onto the skewers, making sure not to crowd them.

When the coals are ready or the gas grill is hot, spray the kabobs on all sides with cooking oil and grill them for 8 to 9 minutes, turning every few minutes, until the vegetables are cooked through and are evenly browned. Transfer the skewers to a platter and let them cool. Line a serving bowl with the lettuce leaves.

When the sausage and veggies are cool, de-skewer them into a large mixing bowl. Add the artichoke hearts, white beans, parsley, basil, and dressing and toss together. Transfer to the lettuce-lined serving bowl and serve.

Grilled Polenta

Polenta is a great side to serve when you are doing some serious grilling. Early in the day, you prepare it on the stove and then spread it in a pan, where you let it sit in a quiet place to meditate as you take care of the rest of the meal. Then, when the grill is hot, it's just a matter of cutting it into squares and giving it 5 minutes over the heat. Fit the polenta squares around the outer edge of the grill or, if you are cooking meat, you can throw them on the while the meat is resting. **Serves 8**

Ingredients

4 cups canned chicken broth

1 teaspoon salt

1 cup polenta

2 tablespoons butter

1 cup grated Parmesan cheese

Olive oil, for brushing

→ **In** a large saucepan over high heat, bring the chicken broth to a boil, and add the salt. Add the polenta in a slow, steady stream, stirring gently as you do. As soon as some bubbles appear, immediately lower the heat to medium-low and start stirring. You must stir continuously while the polenta is cooking.

Continue cooking and stirring for 25 minutes. Add the butter and Parmesan and continue to stir until they are incorporated.

Carefully pour the hot polenta into an oiled 9-by-13-inch baking pan, and spread it out evenly with a rubber spatula. Let it sit at room temperature for up to 6 hours, draped with a clean kitchen cloth.

When ready to grill, cut the polenta into roughly 2-inch squares. Brush both sides with olive oil. Grill for about 5 minutes, turning once, until both sides have nice grill marks and are just heated through. Serve immediately.

Grilled Sweet Potatoes

Simmer these slowly to keep them from getting mushy. Then you need to grill them for only a few minutes before serving. **Serves** 4

Ingredients

4 medium sweet potatoes

½ cup (1 stick) butter, melted

3 tablespoons honey

1 teaspoon ground cinnamon

¼ teaspoon freshly grated nutmeg

Salt and freshly ground black pepper

→ **Peel** the sweet potatoes and cut them lengthwise into ¾-inch-thick slices. Bring 3 quarts of water to a boil and add the sweet potato slices. Simmer until they are just starting to soften, about 12 minutes. Drain and let cool in a single layer on a large platter.

Combine the butter, honey, cinnamon, and nutmeg in a small saucepan and place over low heat, stirring to combine. Brush the potato slices on both sides with the butter mixture and season to taste with salt and pepper.

Prepare enough coals for a medium-hot charcoal fire, or preheat your gas grill on medium-high for 10 minutes with the lid closed.

When the coals are ready or the gas grill is hot, grill the sweet potato slices for about 6 minutes, turning once, until they are soft through the middle and nicely browned.

Classic Coleslaw

You can't have barbecue without coleslaw. It's just part of the equation.
Serves 8

Ingredients

One 16-ounce bag coleslaw mix

2 tablespoons diced onion

½ cup grated radishes

½ cup mayonnaise

¼ cup sour cream

3 tablespoons vegetable oil

3 tablespoons sugar

1 tablespoon white vinegar

1 teaspoon salt

½ teaspoon celery seeds

→ **Combine** the coleslaw mix, onion, and grated radish in a large bowl.

Whisk together the mayonnaise, sour cream, vegetable oil, sugar, vinegar, salt, and celery seeds in a medium bowl. Pour the dressing over the coleslaw mix and toss to coat. Chill for at least 2 hours before serving.

Potato Packets

Fit these in the empty spaces on the grill and you'll have perfect potatoes to go with your meal. Keep in mind that they take 40 minutes, and time the rest of the meal accordingly. **Serves** 4

Ingredients

8 slices bacon (see Note)

1 medium onion, thinly sliced

4 large potatoes, scrubbed and thinly sliced

4 tablespoons (½ stick) butter

Salt and freshly ground black pepper

2 tablespoons olive oil

→ **Lay** out a double layer of aluminum foil about 14 inches long. Place 1 slice of bacon in the center, then 2 slices of onion, then about half a potato's worth of potato slices. Top with ½ tablespoon of butter and season to taste with salt and pepper. Repeat the layering to make a second pile on top of the first. Drizzle ½ tablespoon of olive oil over everything. Fold the foil over the top with a double fold to make a seal, then fold up the sides.

Assemble 3 more packets in the same way.

Place each potato packet on the grill over medium-high heat for about 40 minutes, or until the potatoes are cooked through. You'll have to open one of the packets to check—it's the only way I've figured out to see if they are done. Be careful of the escaping steam.

Note: *You can make these without the bacon if it conflicts with the rest of the meal.*

Roasted Potatoes

These potatoes are preboiled, so they need only a few minutes on the grill to finish cooking. This extra step guarantees that you will have a perfect and worry–free potato accompaniment. **Serves 4 to 6**

Ingredients

1½ pounds new potatoes, preferably fingerling

3 tablespoons extra virgin olive oil

¼ cup chopped garlic

1 tablespoon chopped fresh or dried rosemary

**1 tablespoon chopped fresh thyme,
  or 1 teaspoon dried**

Salt and freshly ground black pepper

→ **Wash** the potatoes well and cut any particularly large ones in half so they are all about the same size. Place the potatoes in a medium saucepan and cover with water. Bring to a boil, then reduce the heat, cover, and cook for 12 minutes, until the potatoes are just tender.

Immediately drain the potatoes and spread them on a sheet pan to cool (if you put them in a bowl, the ones on the bottom will continue cooking until they turn to mush).

Before grilling, transfer the cooled potatoes to a large bowl. Add the olive oil, garlic, rosemary, thyme, and salt and pepper to taste, and mix so the potatoes are evenly coated.

Arrange the potatoes on the grill around whatever else you are cooking, and grill for 10 minutes, turning them at least once. Transfer to a platter and serve.

Note: *If you are cooking meat that needs to rest once it comes off the grill, you can put the potatoes on then if that's easier, or if there's not enough room on the grill grate.*

Mac & Cheese

The Progeny think they know mac and cheese, but this recipe takes it to a whole new level. It's like going from T–ball to fast pitch. You may have to make this one time for dinner, after which the kids will be addicted. Then, when you need them to take it out of the oven because you are manning the grill, they will be more than agreeable.

Serves 6 to 8

Ingredients

1 pound elbow macaroni

4 cups milk

6 tablespoons unsalted butter

½ cup unbleached all-purpose flour

1 pound extra-sharp yellow Cheddar cheese, grated (about 4 cups)

1 tablespoon salt

½ teaspoon freshly ground black pepper

½ teaspoon ground nutmeg

1½ cups crushed potato chips

→ **Preheat** the oven to 375°F.

Bring a large pot of salted water to a boil. Add the macaroni, and cook according to the package instructions for al dente—about 6 minutes. Drain well and set aside.

Heat the milk in a medium saucepan until it just starts bubbling around the edge of the pan. Immediately remove it from the heat without letting it boil. Melt the butter in a large pot and add the flour all at once. Cook over low heat for 2 minutes, stirring with a whisk. Whisk in the hot milk and cook for a minute or two more, stirring continuously, until the mixture thickens and gets smooth. Remove the pan from the heat and stir in the Cheddar, salt, pepper,

and nutmeg. Add the cooked macaroni and stir well. Pour into a 3-quart (9-by-13-inch) baking dish.

Sprinkle the crushed potato chips evenly over the top of the casserole. Bake in the center of the oven for 30 to 35 minutes, or until the sauce is bubbly and the macaroni is lightly browned on top.

Let cool for a few minutes while you alert The Progeny that they won't get any until they _____ (add chore of your choice).

Fragrant Rice

This dish has a wonderful Indian flavor that comes from the combination of cinnamon and cardamom. Though it's slightly exotic, it goes perfectly well with grilled meats and fish. You may have to buy a small container of cardamom seeds for this, but once you taste this rice, it'll become part of the regular rotation and you'll use those seeds up fast. **Serves 4**

Ingredients

1¼ cups basmati or jasmine rice

2 tablespoons vegetable oil

1 small onion, finely chopped

2 pods green cardamom

2 whole cloves

½ teaspoon ground cinnamon

½ teaspoon ground cumin

1 teaspoon salt, or to taste

1½ cups chicken broth

1 cup water

¼ cup golden raisins

½ cup slivered almonds

→ **Place** the rice in a small bowl with enough water to cover. Set aside to soak for 20 minutes.

Heat the oil in a large pot or saucepan over medium heat. Add the onion and sauté until brown, about 6 minutes. Add the cardamom, cloves, cinnamon, and cumin and cook for 1 minute more.

Drain the rice and stir it into the pot. Cook and stir for a few minutes, until the rice is lightly toasted. Add the salt, broth, water, raisins, and almonds to the pot and bring to a boil. Cover and reduce the heat to low. Simmer for about 15 minutes, or until all of the water has been absorbed.

Let stand for 5 minutes, then fluff with a fork before serving.

Baked Brown Rice Pilaf

This rice dish solves a lot of problems for dad. It uses brown rice, which means it's on the healthful side. It's baked, which means you have a little more margin for error than if you were to cook it on the stovetop. And it has a spectacular taste that is not overwhelming, so it can go with a wide variety of grilled meats and fish. **Serves 6**

Ingredients

1 tablespoon extra virgin olive oil

1 tablespoon butter

1 small onion, diced

½ cup carrots, cut into ¼-inch dice

½ cup celery, cut into ¼-inch dice

3 cloves garlic, minced

1½ cups long-grain brown rice, preferably basmati

½ teaspoon dried thyme

⅓ cup raisins

¼ cup chopped pecans

1 teaspoon salt

3 cups chicken broth

→ **Preheat** the oven to 350°F. In a Dutch oven, heat the oil and butter over medium heat. Add the onion, carrots, celery, garlic, and rice and sauté, stirring frequently, until some of the grains are quite brown, about 4 minutes. Add the thyme, raisins, pecans, and salt and cook for 1 minute more.

Carefully add the broth, as it will steam up. Stir, cover the pot, and bake in the preheated oven for 1 hour.

Remove from the oven and fluff the rice with a fork. Cover the pot with a clean kitchen towel and let stand for 5 minutes. Fluff again before serving.

Backyard Beans

These beans are the real deal. They're perfect with any of the smoked meats, burgers, brats, or hot dogs. The Progeny might like them so much that the grilled rib-eyes become an excuse to have something to go with the beans. **Serves 6 to 8**

Ingredients

½ **cup ketchup**

½ **cup dark brown sugar**

2 **tablespoons brown mustard**

2 **tablespoons chili powder**

1 **teaspoon ground cumin**

One 14-ounce can kidney beans, drained

One 14-ounce can pinto beans, drained

One 14-ounce can black-eyed peas, drained

1 **tablespoon extra virgin olive oil**

1 **medium onion, finely chopped**

4 **ounces andouille or other spicy smoked sausage, cut into ½-inch rounds**

4 **cloves garlic, finely chopped**

➜ **In** a large bowl, combine the ketchup, brown sugar, mustard, chili powder, ground cumin, kidney beans, pinto beans, and black-eyed peas and stir together briefly. Set aside, or cover and refrigerate for up to 1 day.

Prepare enough coals for a two-tiered fire, hot on one side and medium on the other, or preheat your gas grill on high on one side and medium on the other for 10 minutes with the lid closed. Remove the bean mixture from the refrigerator.

When the coals are ready or the gas grill is hot, place a large skillet on the hot side of the grill. Add the olive oil and onion and cook, stirring

often, until the onion softens, about 5 minutes. Add the sausage and garlic and cook for 1 minute more.

Carefully add the bean mixture to the skillet and stir to combine. When the liquid comes to a boil, transfer the skillet to the cooler side of the grill. Cover the skillet and the grill and cook for about 12 minutes, stirring a few times and rotating the skillet to make sure the side nearest to the heat isn't burning. Remove the skillet, transfer the beans to a serving bowl, and serve.

Note: *You can also assemble these on the stovetop earlier in the day if that's easier.*

Roasted Corn with Chipotle Butter

An experienced grill man can always find a little empty space on the grill for some ears of corn. Don't be afraid to snap the ears in half if you have to. Of course, grilled corn is great just the way it is, but the chipotle butter gives it an extra kick.

Makes 6 ears

Ingredients

½ **cup butter (1 stick), softened**

2 **chipotle chiles in adobo,
   seeds removed and finely chopped**

1 **teaspoon minced garlic**

½ **teaspoon salt**

½ **teaspoon freshly ground black pepper**

6 **ears corn, husked**

→ **In** a small bowl, use a fork to mash together the butter, chipotles, garlic, salt, and pepper until just combined. Transfer the mixture to a 12-inch piece of plastic wrap and use the wrap to roll the butter mixture into a log roughly the size of the original stick of butter. Place the butter in the refrigerator until ready to use.

Grill the corn over medium-high heat for 10 to 12 minutes, turning frequently as the bottoms begin to turn a golden brown.

Serve immediately, with the chipotle butter on the side.

Roasted Corn & Sweet Onion Salad

This is the perfect way to use up leftover grilled corn. It is also the perfect way to use up the extra corn you purposefully grilled just so you would have it the next day to make this salad. On a serious note, using up leftovers is an important lesson for Dad to pass on to The Progeny. Food should be thrown out only as a last resort. Let the kids see you transform last night's leftovers into sustenance for the following day.

Serves 4

Ingredients

¼ cup plus 2 tablespoons
    extra virgin olive oil

1 medium-sized sweet onion,
    thinly sliced

Kernels cut from 6 ears grilled corn,
    or two 8-ounce cans corn kernels
    packed in water, drained

One 6-ounce jar roasted red peppers,
    drained and finely chopped

½ cup diced celery (¼-inch dice)

½ cup finely chopped fresh parsley

2 tablespoons fresh lemon juice

2 tablespoons red wine vinegar

2 tablespoons chopped fresh basil,
    or 1 teaspoon dried

1 tablespoon fresh thyme leaves,
    or 1 teaspoon dried

1 teaspoon sugar

1 teaspoon salt

Freshly ground black pepper

→ **Place** a large, heavy-bottomed skillet over medium heat. When the pan gets hot, add 2 tablespoons of the oil, spreading it so it evenly coats the bottom of the pan. Add the onions and cook, stirring regularly, until they start to brown, about 8 minutes. Remove from the heat and transfer to a mixing bowl.

Add the corn to the bowl, along with the roasted peppers, celery, and parsley.

In a small bowl, whisk together the lemon juice, vinegar, basil, thyme, sugar, salt, and pepper to taste. Slowly drizzle in the remaining ¼ cup olive oil. Pour the dressing over the vegetables and serve, or refrigerate for up to 8 hours.

Note: *Instead of sautéing the onions, you can also grill them, following the instructions on page 174.*

Guacamole

A Dad has an obligation to make perfect guacamole. The trick is a little more lime juice and a little more salt than you think you may need. It's a fine balance. But this is a good lesson in seasoning and tasting. Add a pinch of salt, a teaspoon more lime, stir it well into the guac, and taste. Repeat until it's exactly the way you want it.

Makes about 1¼ cups

Ingredients

2 ripe avocados

2 Roma tomatoes, seeded and cut into ½-inch dice

¼ cup finely chopped red onion

¼ cup chopped fresh cilantro

¼ cup fresh lime juice (2 to 3 limes), plus more if needed

3 tablespoons finely chopped garlic

1 teaspoon salt, plus more if needed

Several dashes hot sauce

Tortilla chips, for serving

→ Cut each avocado in half lengthwise, remove the pit, and scoop out the meat into a medium bowl. Mash the avocado with a potato masher or the back of a fork. Add the tomatoes, onion, cilantro, lime juice, garlic, salt, and hot sauce and mix together. Adjust the seasoning, and serve immediately with chips.

Note: *If you make the guacamole in advance, lay some plastic wrap directly over the surface of the guacamole, then cover the bowl and refrigerate for up to 12 hours.*

Collard Greens

You'll find these on the steam tables of many barbecue joints, creating that magical vortex at the center of the plate where the barbecue sauce, baked beans, and greens all come together and their flavors coalesce. Don't be afraid of the size and relative toughness of the leaves. If you have a big enough pot, they're a cinch to prepare. You can also leave out the bacon if that makes any of The Progeny happier. Just add a bit more salt. **Serves** 4

Ingredients

2 large bunches collard greens

3 tablespoons extra virgin olive oil

1 onion, sliced

2 cloves garlic, coarsely chopped

2 bay leaves

3 slices thick-cut bacon, cut crosswise into ¼-inch strips

3 cups chicken broth

2 tablespoons apple cider vinegar

1 teaspoon sugar

1 teaspoon salt

Freshly ground black pepper

→ **Cut** away the tough stalks and stems from the collards, and discard any leaves that are bruised or yellow. Wash the collards thoroughly to remove any grit. Dry thoroughly and tear the leaves into large pieces.

Place a large pot over medium heat and add the olive oil. Add the onion, garlic, bay leaves, and bacon. Cook until the onions are soft and starting to brown, about 8 minutes. Shove in the greens, pushing them down into the pot. Add the broth, vinegar, sugar, salt, pepper to taste and enough water to cover the greens. Bring the liquid to a boil, turning the greens over occasionally with a wooden spoon as they wilt. Reduce the heat to low and simmer, covered, for 1 hour, until the greens are quite soft.

Creamed Spinach

Peter Luger's Steakhouse in Brooklyn is known for its superior steaks, but few order the legendary porterhouse without also getting a side of creamed spinach. Their recipe is a closely guarded secret, but this one comes close to emulating its superlative flavor and texture. **Serves 4**

Ingredients

2 tablespoons unsalted butter

2 tablespoons extra virgin olive oil

3 pounds spinach, stems removed and washed well

2 cloves garlic, finely chopped

¾ cup heavy cream

2 ounces cream cheese

1 teaspoon freshly ground nutmeg

¼ cup freshly grated Parmesan cheese

1 teaspoon sugar

¼ teaspoon cayenne pepper

→ **Heat** the butter and oil in a large, heavy-bottomed pot over medium-high heat, add the spinach and garlic, and cook, stirring continuously, for 2 minutes, until the spinach loses some of its water and the garlic softens.

Add the cream, cream cheese, nutmeg, Parmesan, sugar, and cayenne pepper and stir well. Lower the heat to medium-low and cook until the cream reduces and starts to thicken, about 6 minutes. Serve immediately.

Sweet & Spicy Corn Muffins

These are great to serve with anything that comes with barbecue sauce. They have a touch of sweetness, which I like in my corn muffins, and a bit of heat.

Makes 12 muffins

Ingredients

1 cup unbleached all-purpose flour

1 cup yellow cornmeal

6 tablespoons sugar

1 tablespoon baking powder

1 teaspoon baking soda

1½ teaspoons salt

3 eggs

1 cup sour cream

½ cup (1 stick) butter, melted

1 cup canned corn kernels, drained

One 4-ounce can diced green chiles

½ jalapeño chile, stemmed, seeded, and finely chopped

→ **Preheat** the oven to 350°F. Lightly grease a 12-cup muffin tin.

In a large bowl, whisk together the flour, cornmeal, sugar, baking powder, baking soda, and salt until combined.

In a medium bowl, whisk together the eggs, sour cream, and melted butter. Stir in the corn, green chiles, and jalapeño.

Pour the wet ingredients into the dry and stir until just combined. Do not overmix. Fill each muffin cup three-fourths full of batter. Bake on the center rack of the oven until a toothpick stuck into the center of the center muffin comes out clean, 18 to 20 minutes.

Let the muffins cool in the pan on a rack, then run a small knife around the edge of each before inverting the tin and tipping out the muffins.

Skillet Focaccia

This quick and easy bread benefits from the savory top that smothers it with flavor. Serve it pretty much with anything grilled that's not Asian inspired. **Serves 8**

Ingredients

1 tablespoon butter

¼ cup plus 1 tablespoon extra virgin olive oil

2 medium onions, sliced about ¼ inch thick

One 6-ounce jar artichoke hearts in oil, drained and cut into ½-inch pieces

¼ cup sliced kalamata olives

2 tablespoons brown sugar

2 cups unbleached all-purpose flour

1 tablespoon baking powder

1 teaspoon salt

1 teaspoon sugar

1 cup whole milk

1 egg

¼ cup grated Parmesan cheese

→ **Preheat** the oven to 350°F.

Place a large, oven-safe skillet over medium-high heat, add the butter and 1 tablespoon of the oil, and let it get hot, about 2 minutes. Cook the onions, stirring occasionally, until they soften, about 10 minutes. Add the artichoke hearts, olives, and brown sugar and cook for 2 minutes more. Remove from the heat and set aside.

In a large bowl, whisk together the flour, baking powder, salt, and sugar.

In a small bowl, combine the milk, egg, the remaining ¼ cup olive oil, and the Parmesan cheese. Pour the wet ingredients into the dry and stir together until just combined. The dough will be a bit sticky—do not overmix.

Spread the dough over the onion mixture in the skillet and bake on the center rack of the oven until a toothpick inserted into the center comes out clean, 30 to 35 minutes. Let the focaccia cool for 15 minutes, then place a plate over the top and invert the skillet so the onion mixture is on top. Cut into wedges or squares and serve or let it cool completely, wrap well in plastic, and store at room temperature for up to 24 hours.

Note: *To warm up the focaccia, wrap it in foil and place on the coolest part of the grill for 4 to 5 minutes. You can sprinkle more Parmesan on top if you like.*

Double Chocolate Brownies

These are the perfect brownies. They are so good they exonerate Dad for any number of parental missteps, like forgetting to knock or coming home too early or forgetting which dresser drawers are off limits. Just don't overdo it or the brownie mojo will wear out. **Makes 9 brownies**

Ingredients

½ cup (1 stick) butter, cut into 4 pieces

½ cup Dutch-process unsweetened cocoa powder

1 cup granulated sugar

8 ounces semisweet chocolate chips

1 teaspoon pure vanilla extract

2 extra-large eggs

¾ cup unbleached all-purpose flour

Confectioners' sugar, for dusting

→ **Preheat** the oven to 325°F. Grease an 8-by-8-inch baking pan. Place the butter in a small saucepan over medium-low heat and stir continuously until the butter is just melted. Add the cocoa powder. Use a rubber spatula to transfer the cocoa mixture to a large mixing bowl.

Let the cocoa mixture cool for 2 minutes. Then add the granulated sugar, chocolate chips, and vanilla and stir with a wooden spoon until combined. Add the eggs one at a time, stirring so that each is well combined. Add the flour and stir just until combined. Do not overmix. Transfer the batter to the pan and bake on the center rack for 22 minutes, or until a toothpick inserted in the center comes out clean or with tiny crumbs.

Dust with confectioners' sugar, cut into 9 squares, and serve.

Bananas Foster

"Flame on!" Yes, here is Dad's chance to wow the kids with a flaming dessert. The most important part of this technique is to maintain a hot pan so the rum ignites. Make sure you have all the ingredients prepped and easily accessible, as once you start this, you'll have to act fast. After serving this for dessert at dinner, you may find The Progeny asking you to make it again for breakfast the next day.

Serves 4

Ingredients

4 bananas, ripe but not overripe

4 tablespoons (½ stick) butter

6 tablespoons brown sugar

2 ounces rum

½ teaspoon ground cinnamon

4 scoops cold vanilla ice cream

→ **Heat** a 12-inch skillet, preferably cast iron, over a hot grill until smoking.

Meanwhile, peel the bananas and halve them lengthwise. Place the butter in the pan. It should melt and start to brown quickly. Immediately add the brown sugar and stir to form a caramel-looking sauce that is bubbling quickly.

Add the bananas and cinnamon.

Carefully pour in the rum and ignite it with a match or tip the pan slightly to catch the flames from the grill. When the flames subside, toss the bananas carefully to coat them with the sauce and cook for 2 more minutes. Place a scoop of ice cream in each individual bowl, spoon the bananas and sauce over the ice cream, and serve immediately.

Moose Tracks Bread Pudding

When it comes to ice cream, Moose Tracks—vanilla ice cream with chocolate fudge and a hint of marshmallow—is our favorite flavor. I've taken the essence of Moose Tracks and transformed it into this unctuous, chocolaty bread pudding that you can make right on the grill. **Serves 6**

Ingredients

¾ loaf (about 12 ounces) old-fashioned white bread

4 cups whole milk

4 ripe bananas

3 eggs

1 scant cup sugar

1½ tablespoons pure vanilla extract

½ teaspoon freshly grated nutmeg

½ teaspoon ground cinnamon

½ teaspoon salt

8 ounces semisweet chocolate chips

➔ **Stack** up a few slices of bread and cut them into ¾-inch squares. Repeat with the remaining bread slices. Place the cubes in a large bowl and add the milk. Allow to stand for 20 minutes.

In a separate large bowl, mash 3 of the bananas. Add the eggs, sugar, vanilla, nutmeg, cinnamon, and salt. Cut the remaining banana in half lengthwise and then into ½-inch slices. Set aside.

After the bread has soaked, add it along with all the milk to the banana mixture and stir together. Stir in the chocolate chips and banana slices. Turn out into a lightly greased 12-inch cast iron skillet and cover with aluminum foil.

Prepare enough coals for a medium charcoal fire, or preheat one side of your gas grill on medium for 10 minutes with the lid closed.

When the coals are ready or the gas grill is hot, assemble the coals on one side of the coal grate, in a small pile. Place the pan on the grill grate, away from the coals. Cover the grill and cook the bread pudding for 20 minutes. Turn the pan and cook for 20 to 25 minutes more, until the edges are golden and a toothpick inserted in the center comes out nearly clean.

Let cool slightly before serving.

Pear-Apple-Cranberry Crisp

This is the kind of dish most people don't think Dad can make. It's more like something you would see cooling on a farmhouse windowsill. But "quaintly old-fashioned" and "comfy" can be part of Dad's world, too. Just don't wear a gingham apron.

Serves 6

Ingredients

3 cups peeled, cored, and sliced apples

2 cups peeled, cored, and sliced pears

1 cup fresh or frozen cranberries, thawed

½ cup sugar

1 teaspoon ground cinnamon

Pinch ground nutmeg, preferably freshly grated

2 tablespoons fresh lemon juice

½ cup brown sugar

6 tablespoons cold butter, cut in half lengthwise and then into ¼-inch slices

½ cup rolled oats

½ cup unbleached all-purpose flour

½ cup walnuts

Dash salt

→ **Preheat** the oven to 400° F. Lightly grease an 8-inch square baking pan.

Place the apple slices, pear slices, and the cranberries in a large bowl. Add the sugar, ½ teaspoon of the cinnamon, the nutmeg, and lemon juice and mix so the fruit is evenly coated. Place the brown sugar, butter, oats, flour, walnuts, salt, and the remaining ½ teaspoon cinnamon in the bowl of a food processor fitted with the steel blade and pulse a few times until everything is mixed together.

Arrange the fruit mixture in the baking pan. Crumble the topping in an even layer over the top and bake on the center rack until the topping browns lightly, 35 to 40 minutes. Let cool.

Note: *Because the crisp is such a snap to prepare, try to assemble it the morning of the meal. You can assemble the topping the night before. Do not wrap the crisp in plastic, as it will make the topping soggy. Instead, cover it with a clean cloth. By the time you're ready to serve the crisp, the coals will have died down enough that you can place the crisp under the closed grill for a few minutes to warm it up.*

Index

Table of Equivalents

The exact equivalents in the following tables have been rounded for convenience.

Liquid/Dry Measurements

U.S.	Metric
¼ teaspoon	1.25 milliliters
½ teaspoon	2.5 milliliters
1 teaspoon	5 milliliters
1 tablespoon (3 teaspoons)	15 milliliters
1 fluid ounce (2 tablespoons)	30 milliliters
¼ cup	60 milliliters
⅓ cup	80 milliliters
½ cup	120 milliliters
1 cup	240 milliliters
1 pint (2 cups)	480 milliliters
1 quart (4 cups, 32 ounces)	960 milliliters
1 gallon (4 quarts)	3.84 liters
1 ounce (by weight)	28 grams
1 pound	448 grams
2.2 pounds	1 kilogram

Lengths

U.S.	Metric
⅛ inch	3 millimeters
¼ inch	6 millimeters
½ inch	12 millimeters
1 inch	2.5 centimeters

Oven Temperatures

Fahrenheit	Celsius	Gas
250	120	½
275	140	1
300	150	2
325	160	3
350	180	4
375	190	5
400	200	6
425	220	7
450	230	8
475	240	9
500	260	10

Bob Sloan is the celebrated author of the best-selling *Dad's Own Cookbook*. He has also written *The Tailgating Cookbook* and *Great Burgers* and is coauthor of *Hi-Fi's and Hi-Balls* and *A Stiff Drink and a Close Shave* (all from Chronicle Books). His humor pieces and fiction have appeared in *Playboy* magazine. Based in New York City, Sloan is a busy guy who teaches, writes mysteries, and, most important, knows his way around a grill.

Antonis Achilleos is a New York—based photographer whose work has appeared in many magazines as well as in the *Big Fat Cookies* cookbook.

photo by Antonis Achilleos

Also available:

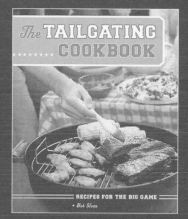

The **TAILGATING COOKBOOK**

RECIPES FOR THE BIG GAME

· Bob Sloan